My First Artist's Book

A compilation of artwork pieces for all artists.

All artworks of this book designed and created by
E. C. Branscom

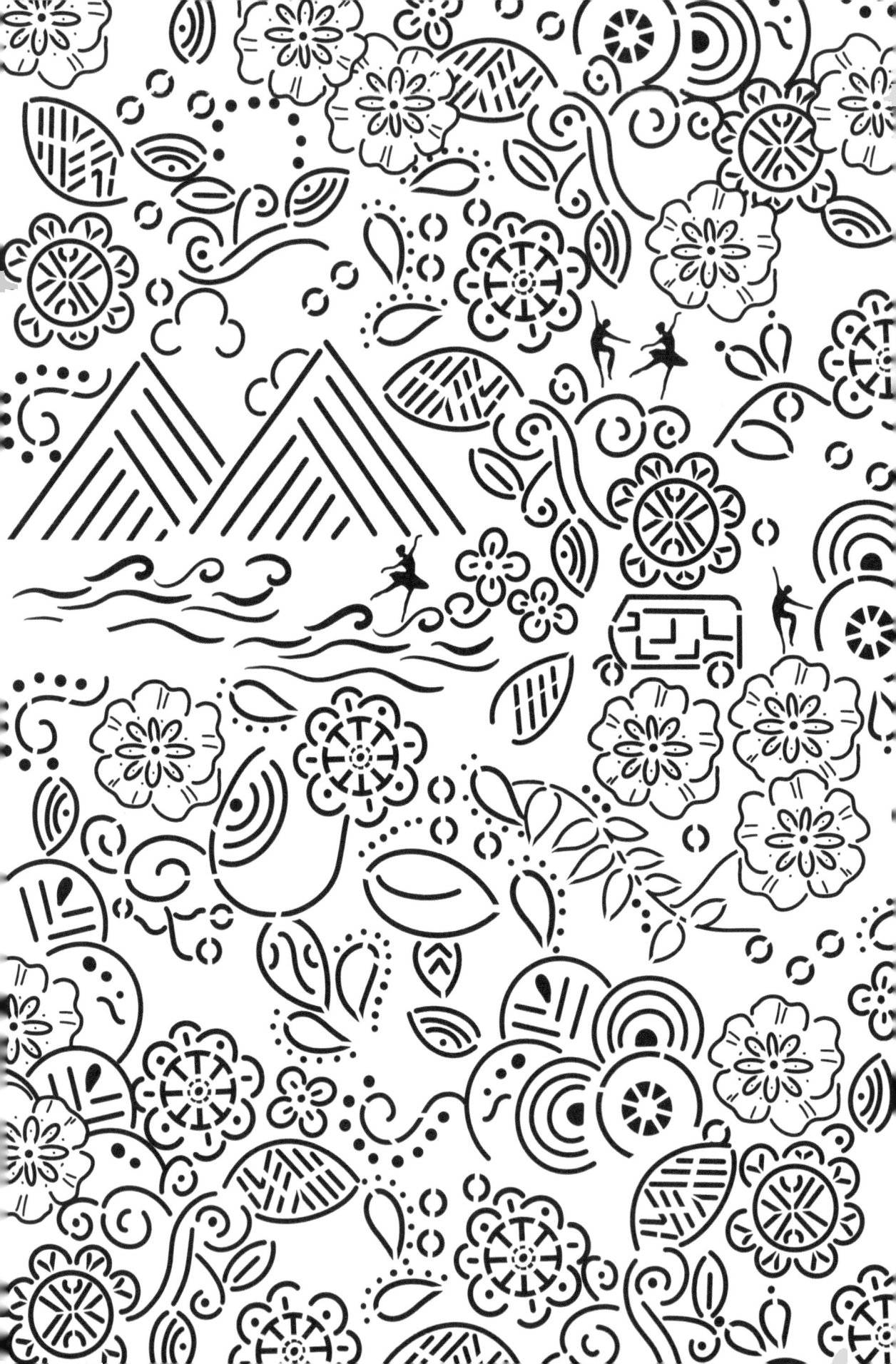

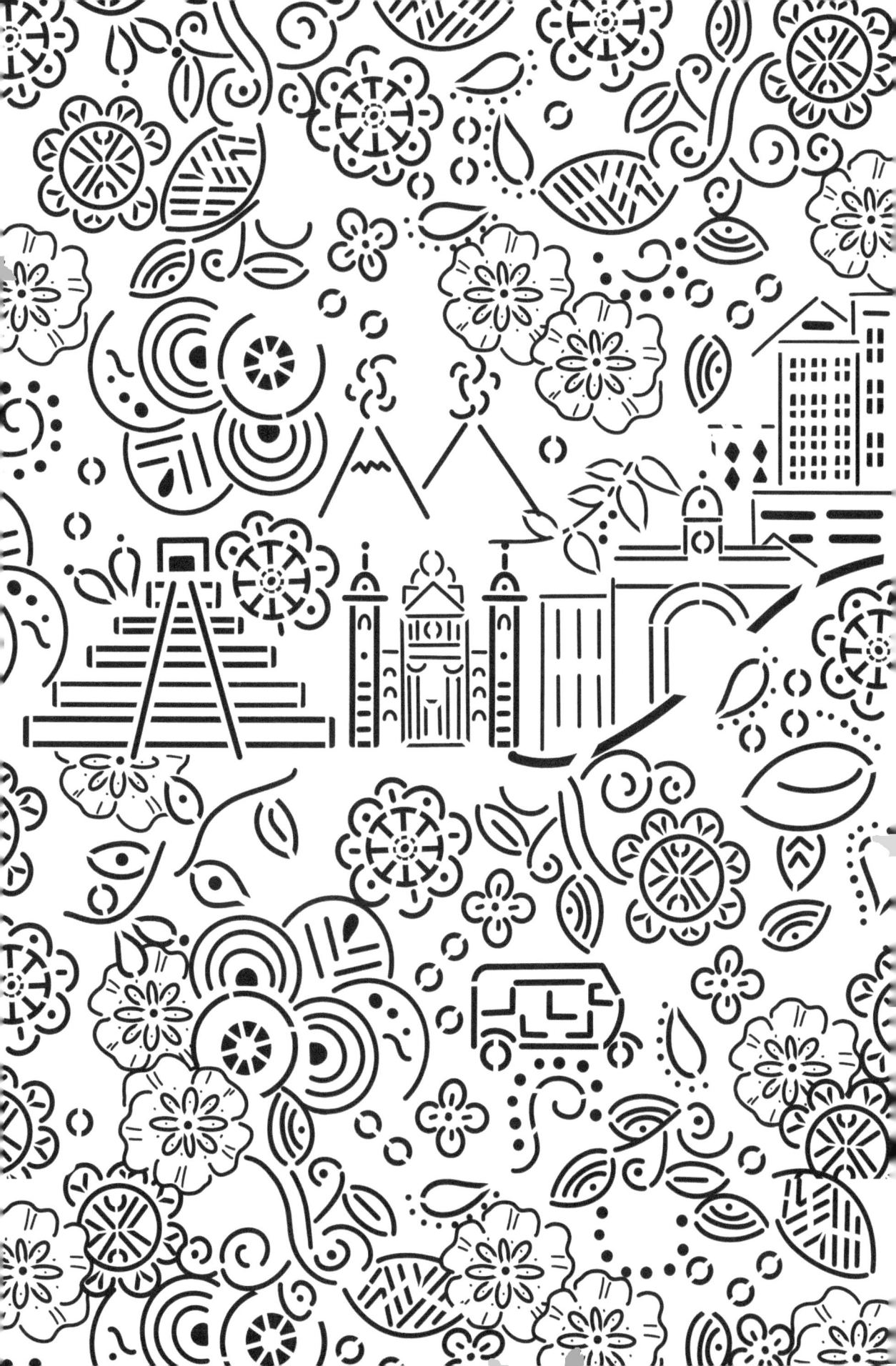

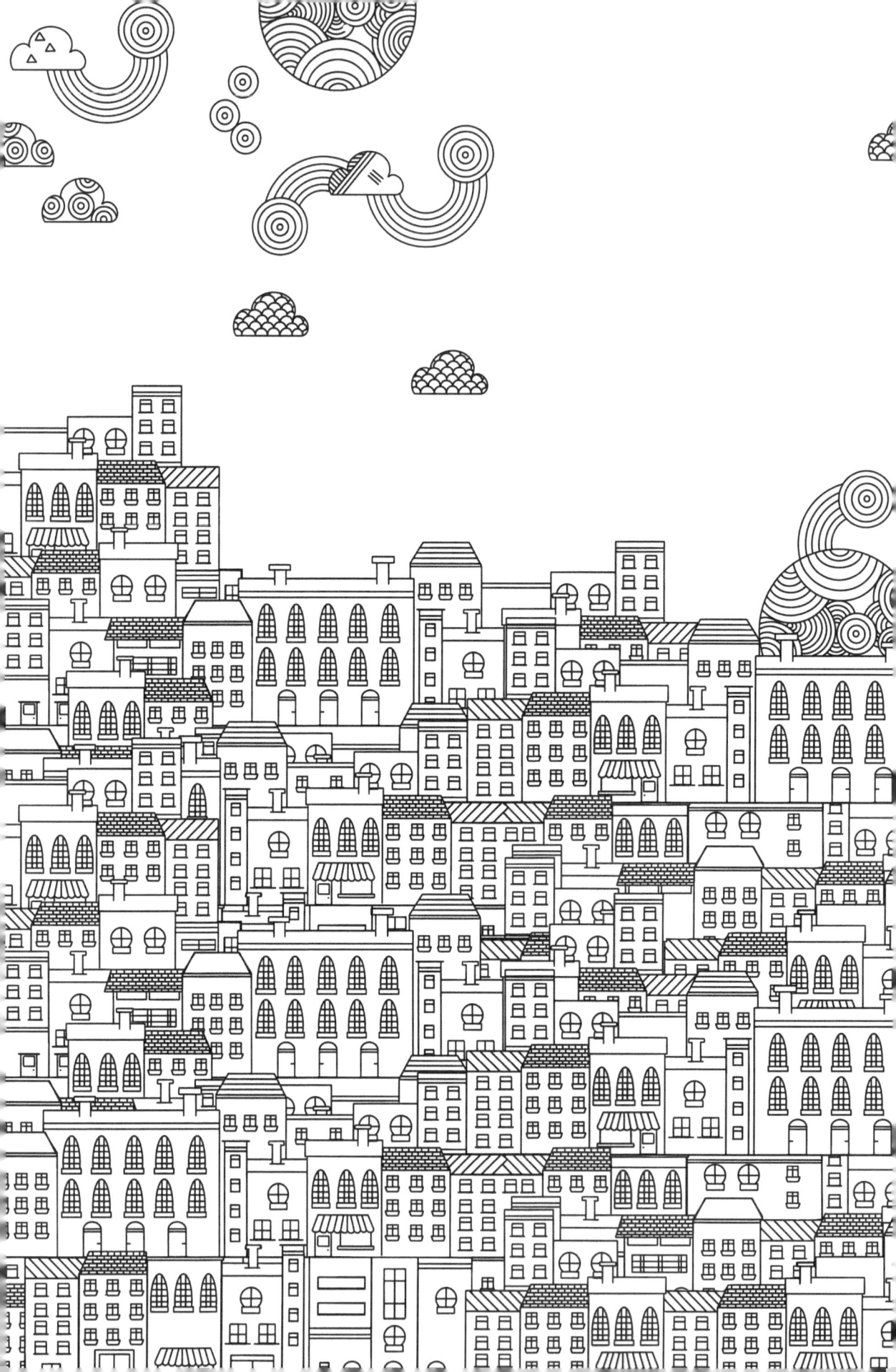

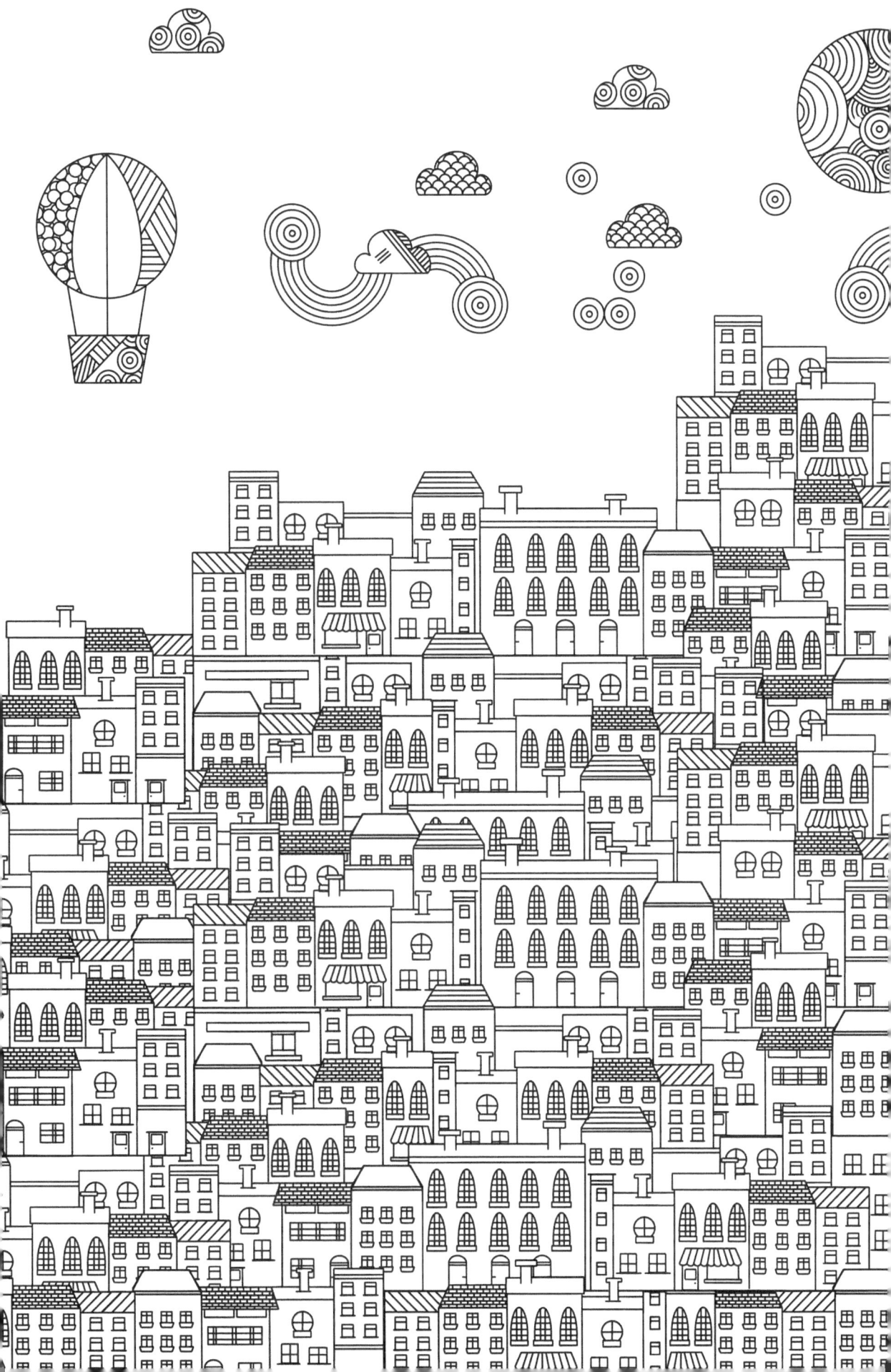

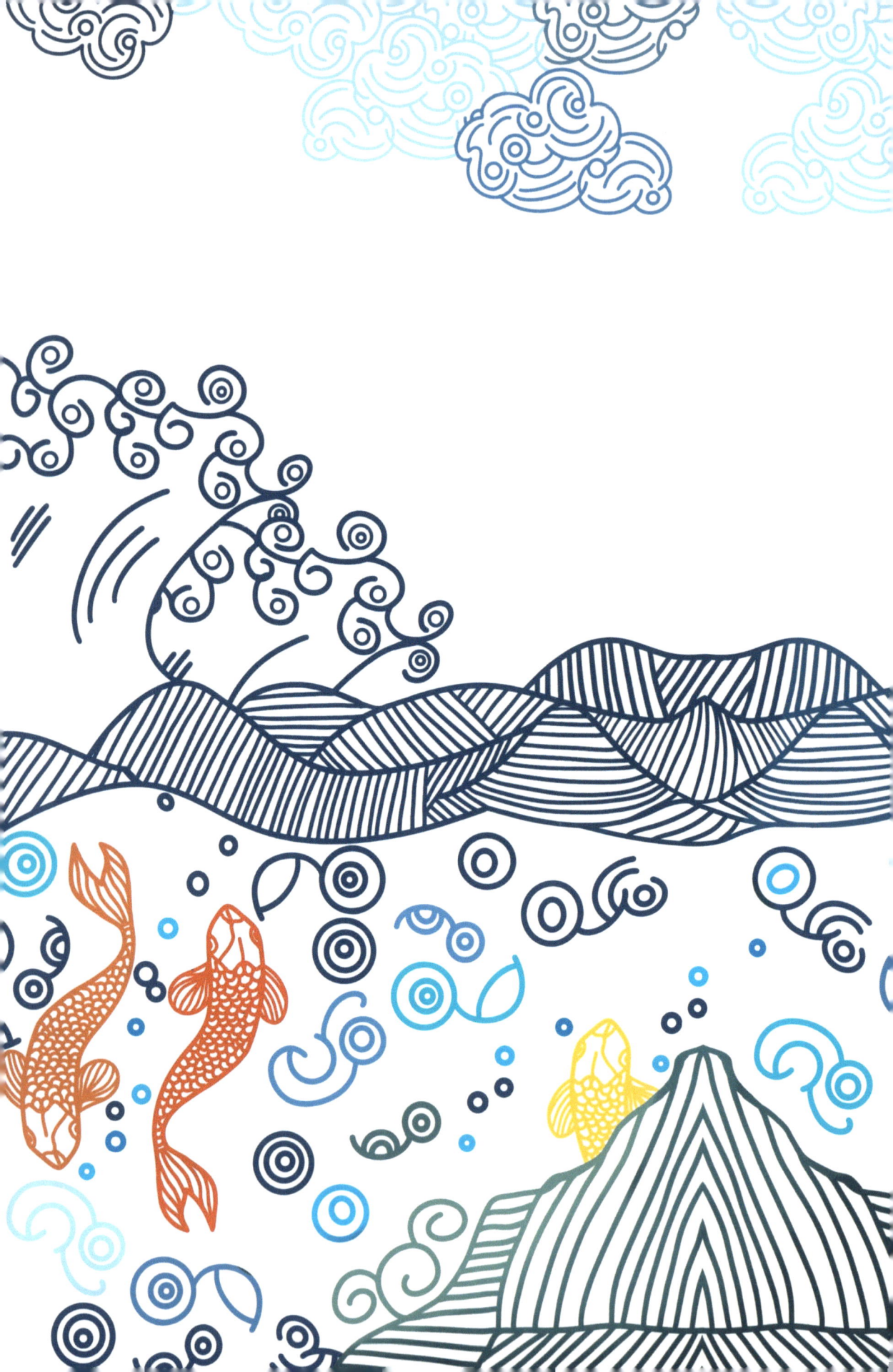

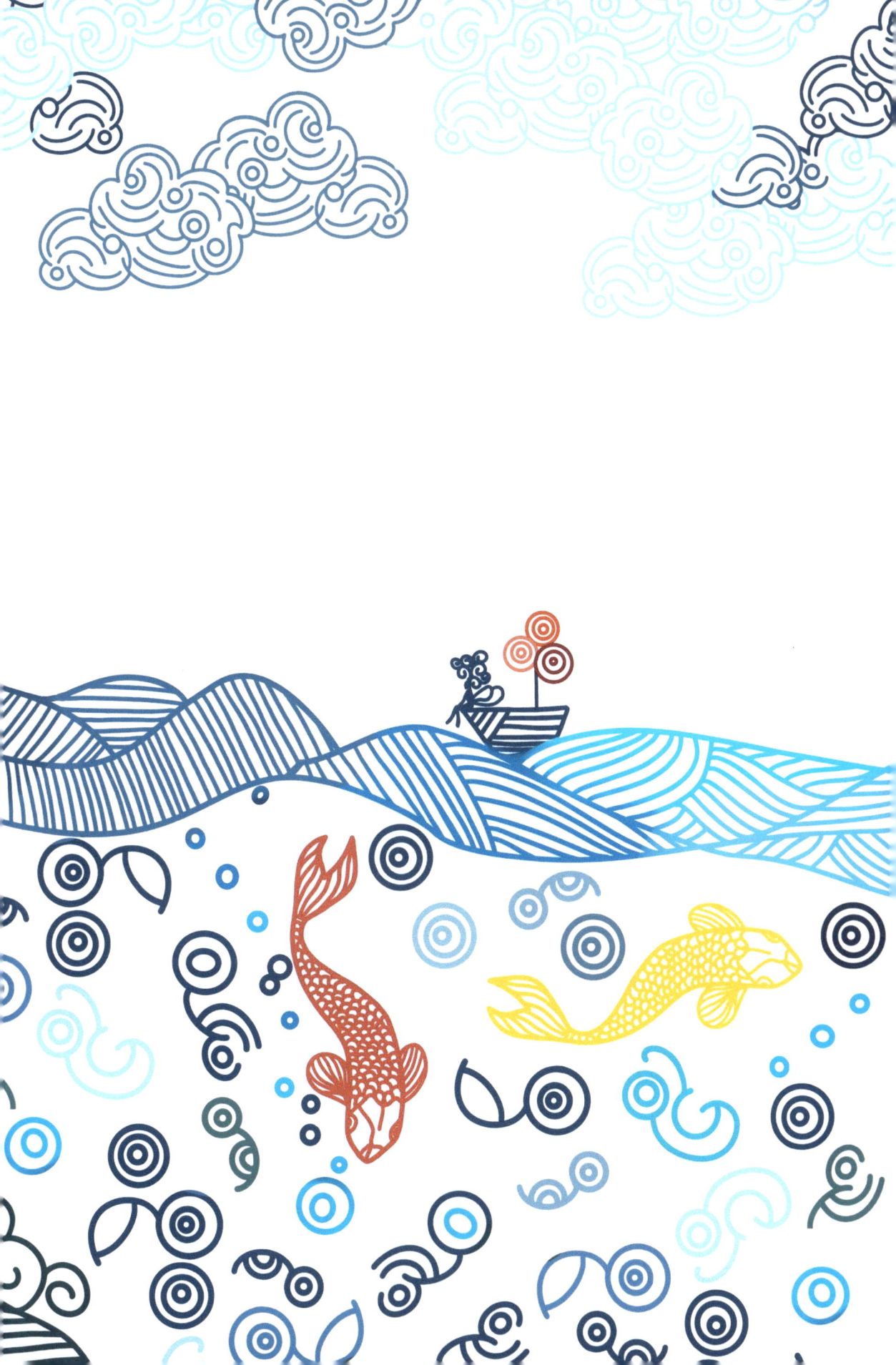

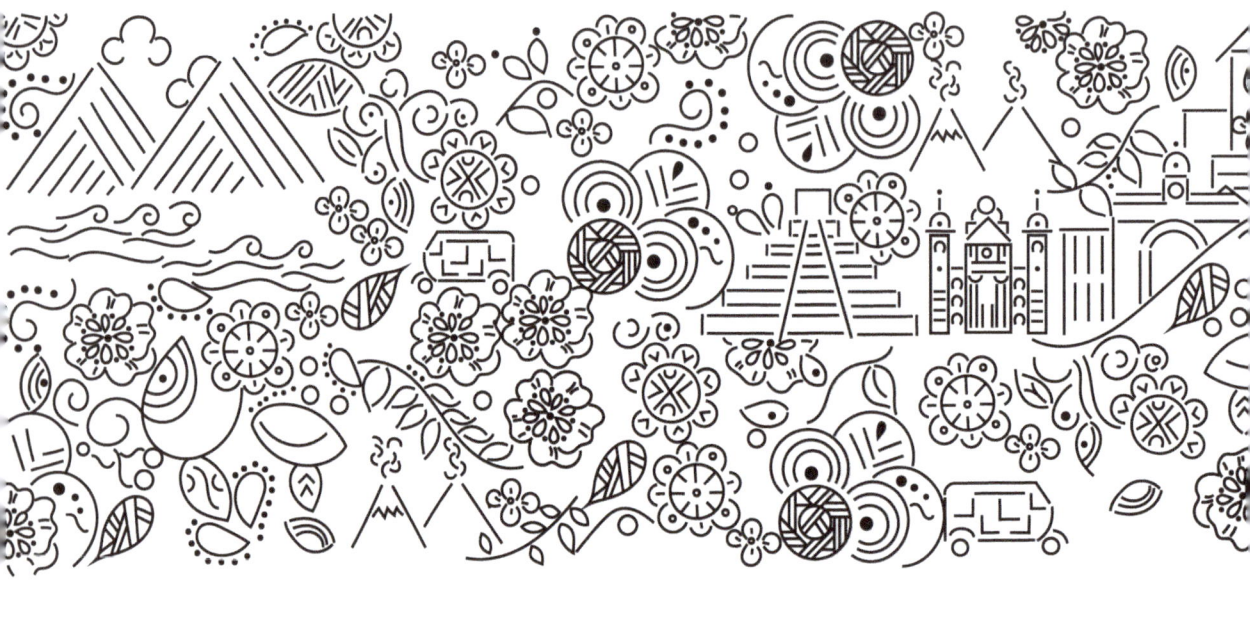

Different designs I made for different contests (I never won any in any category but I learned a lot from the experience).

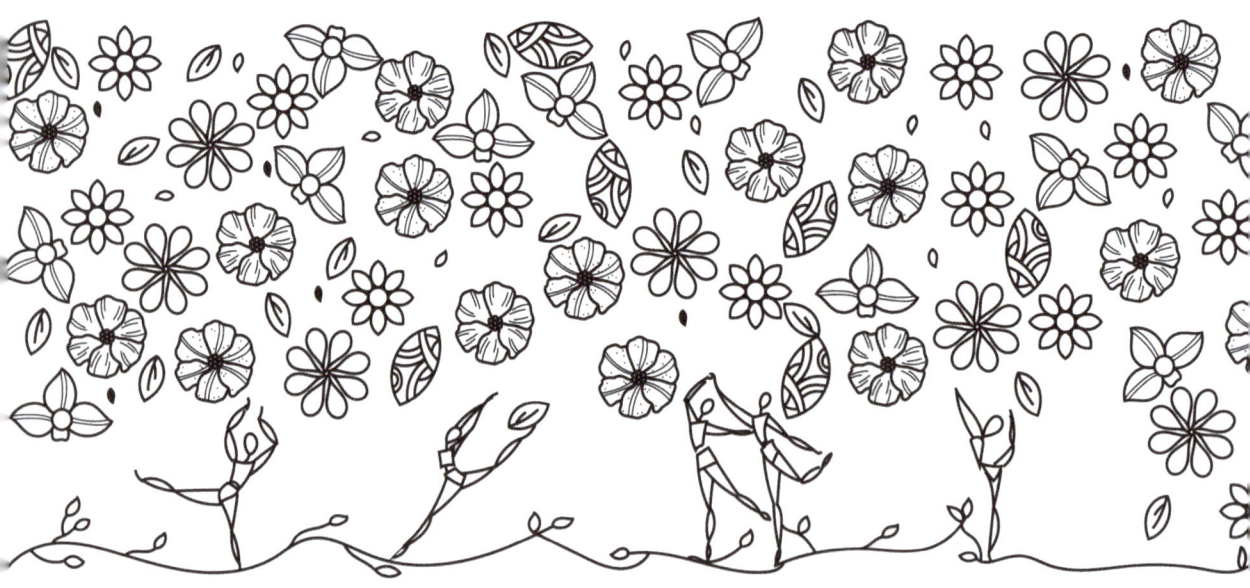

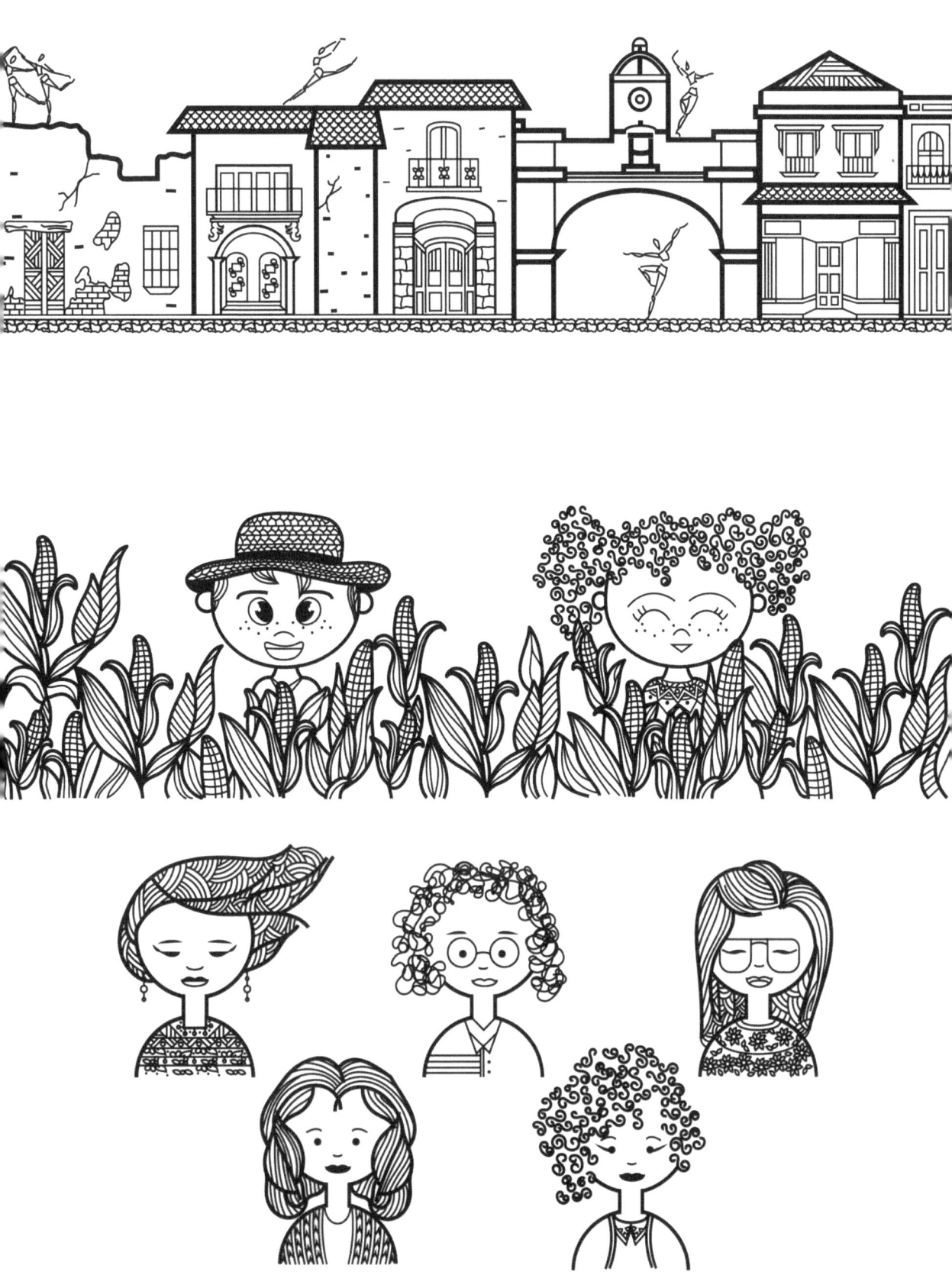

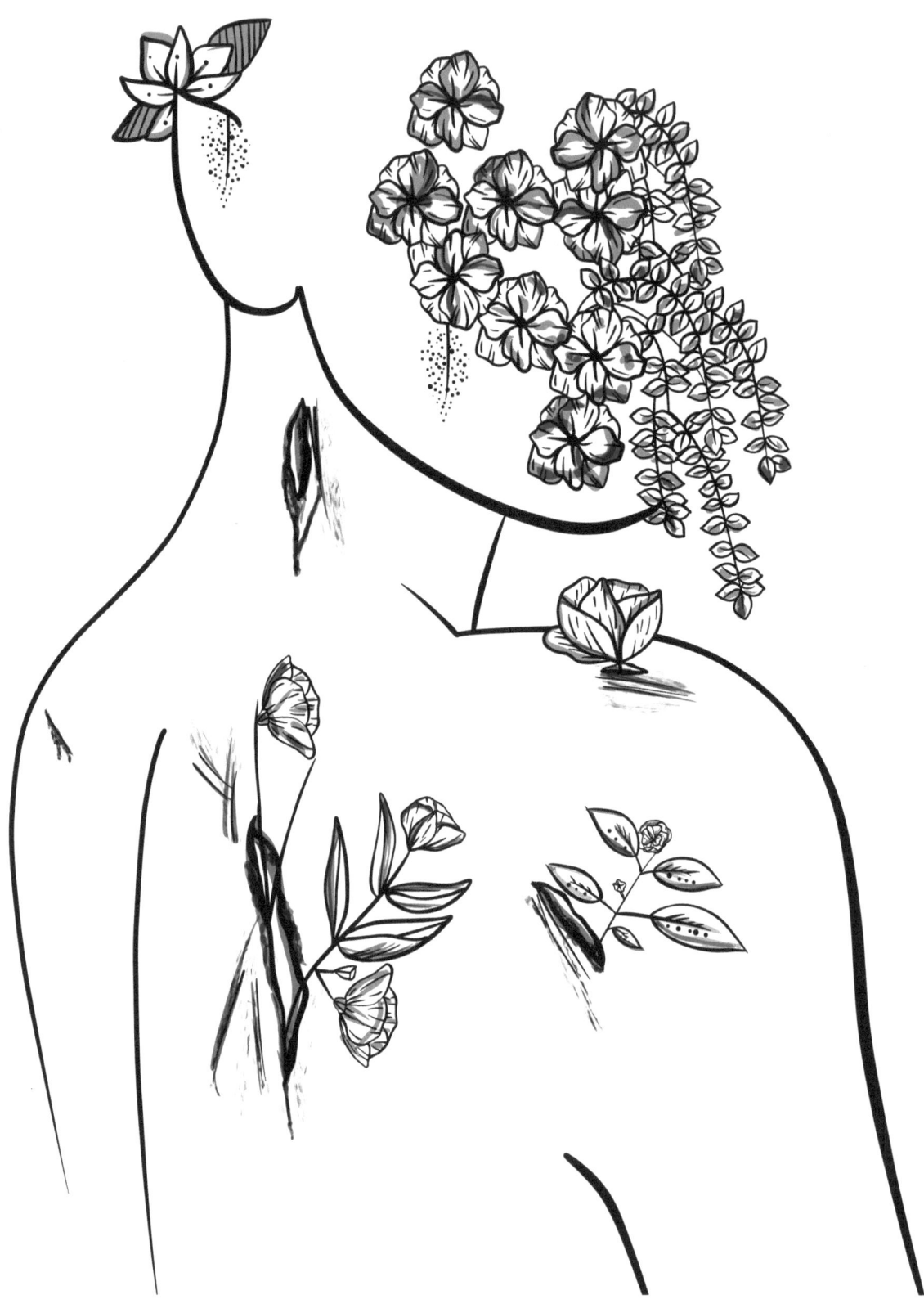

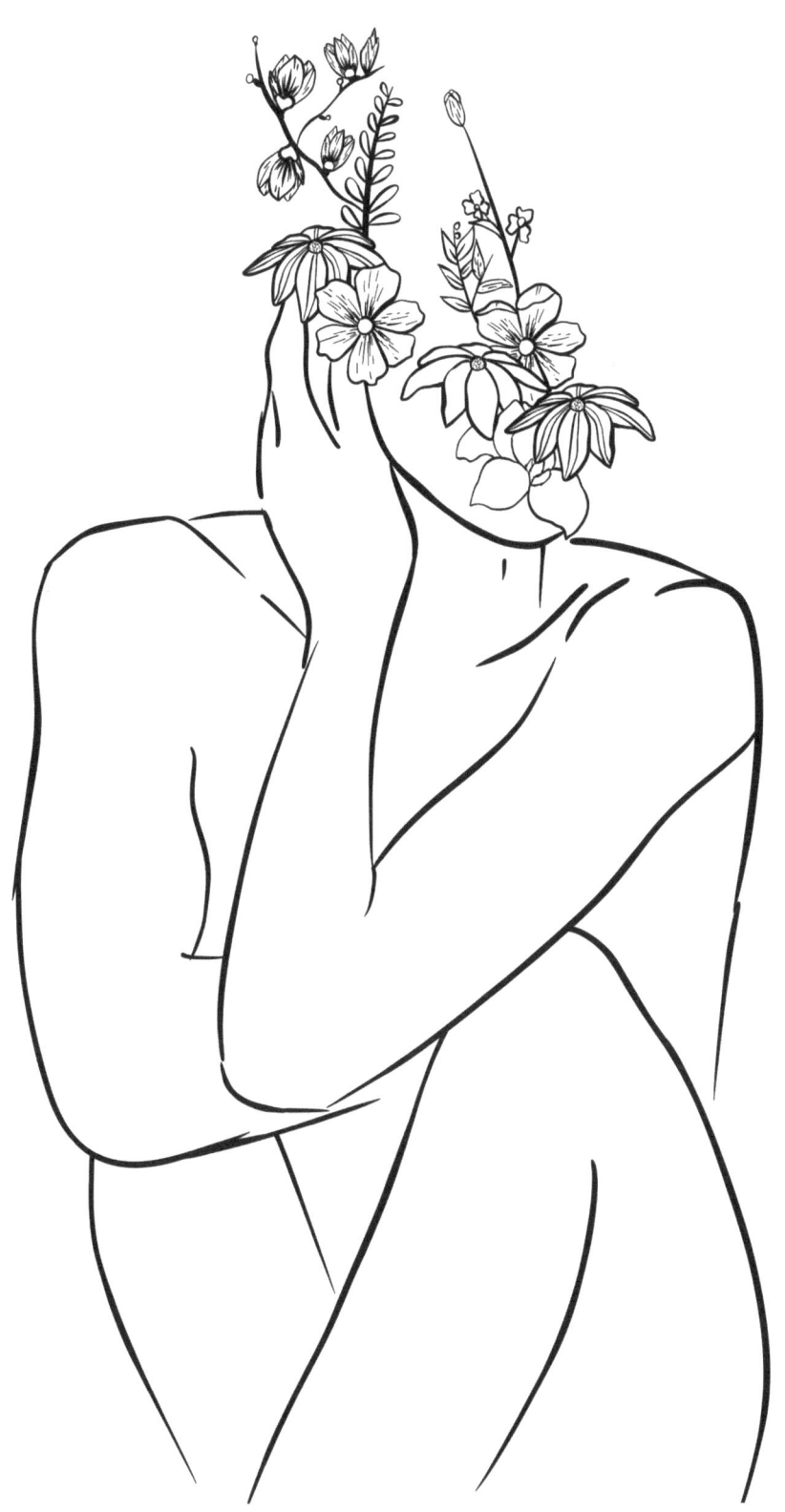

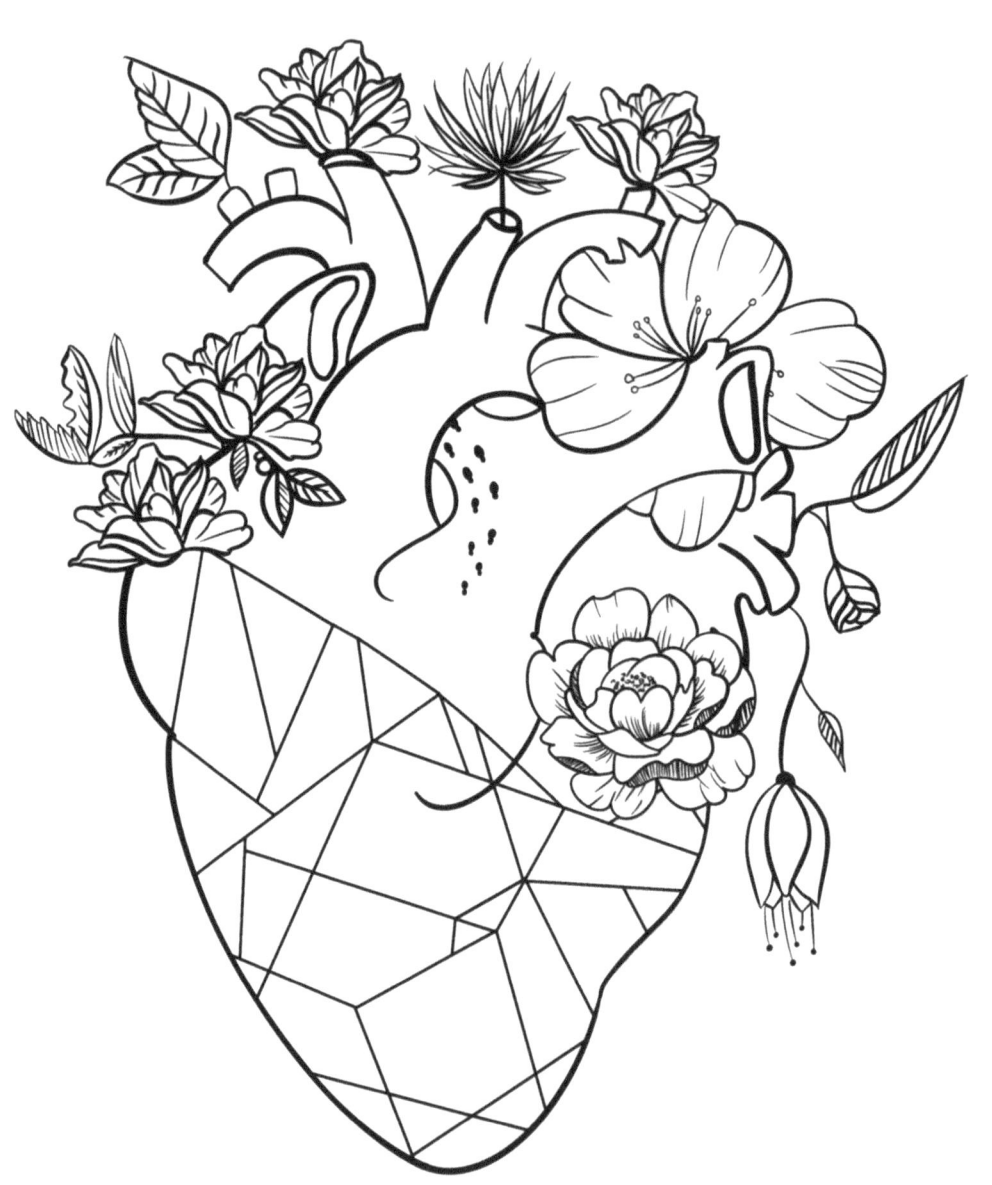

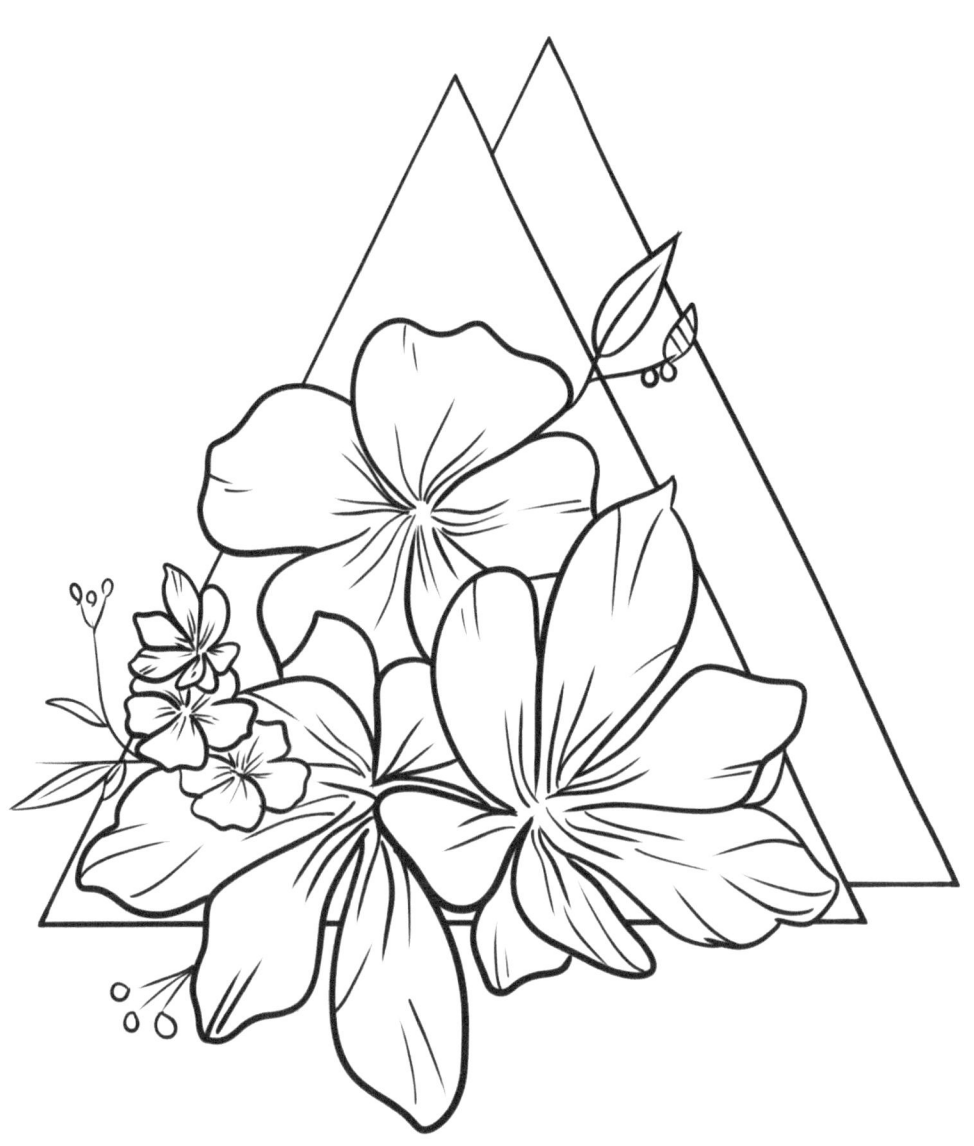

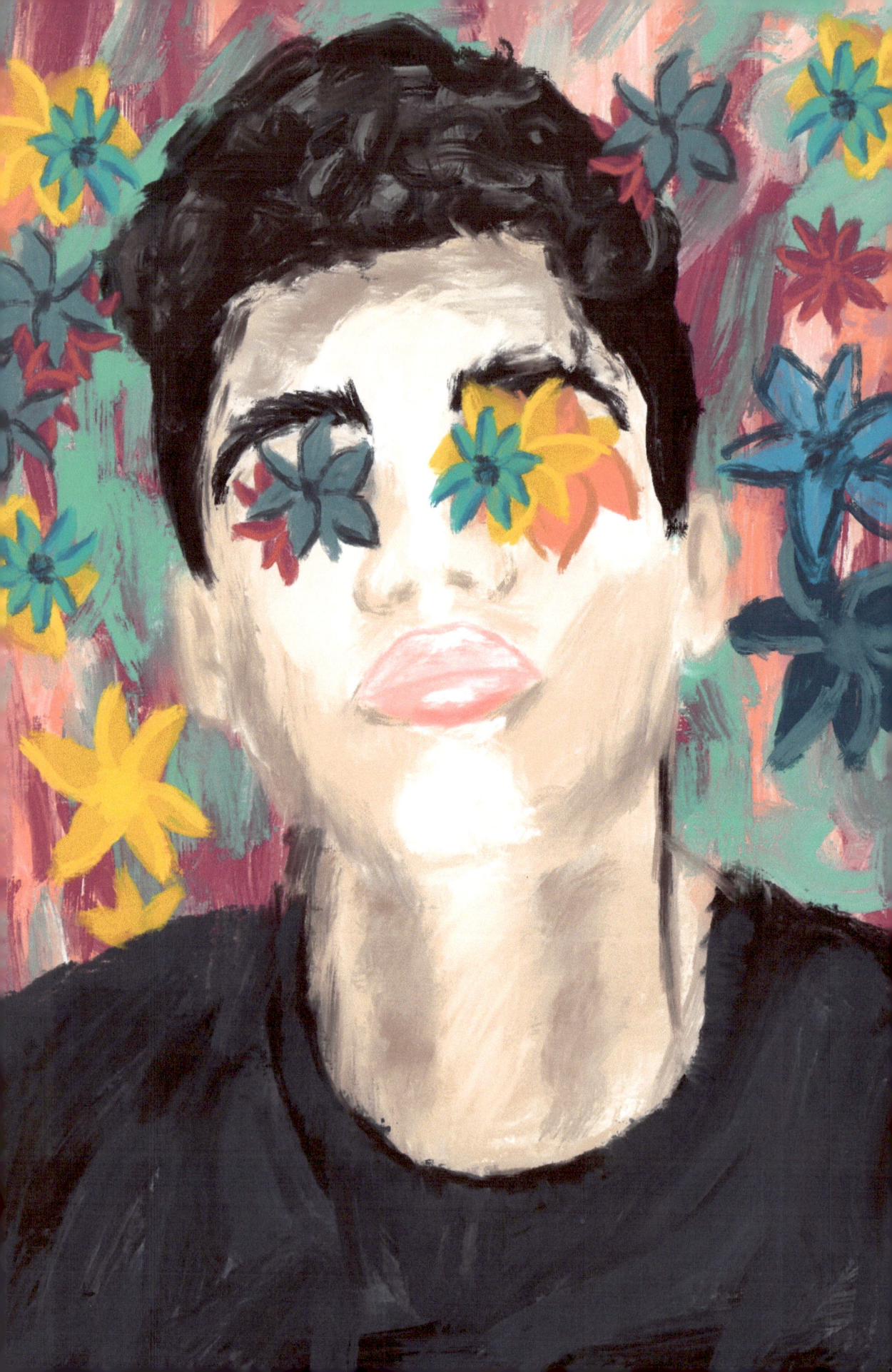

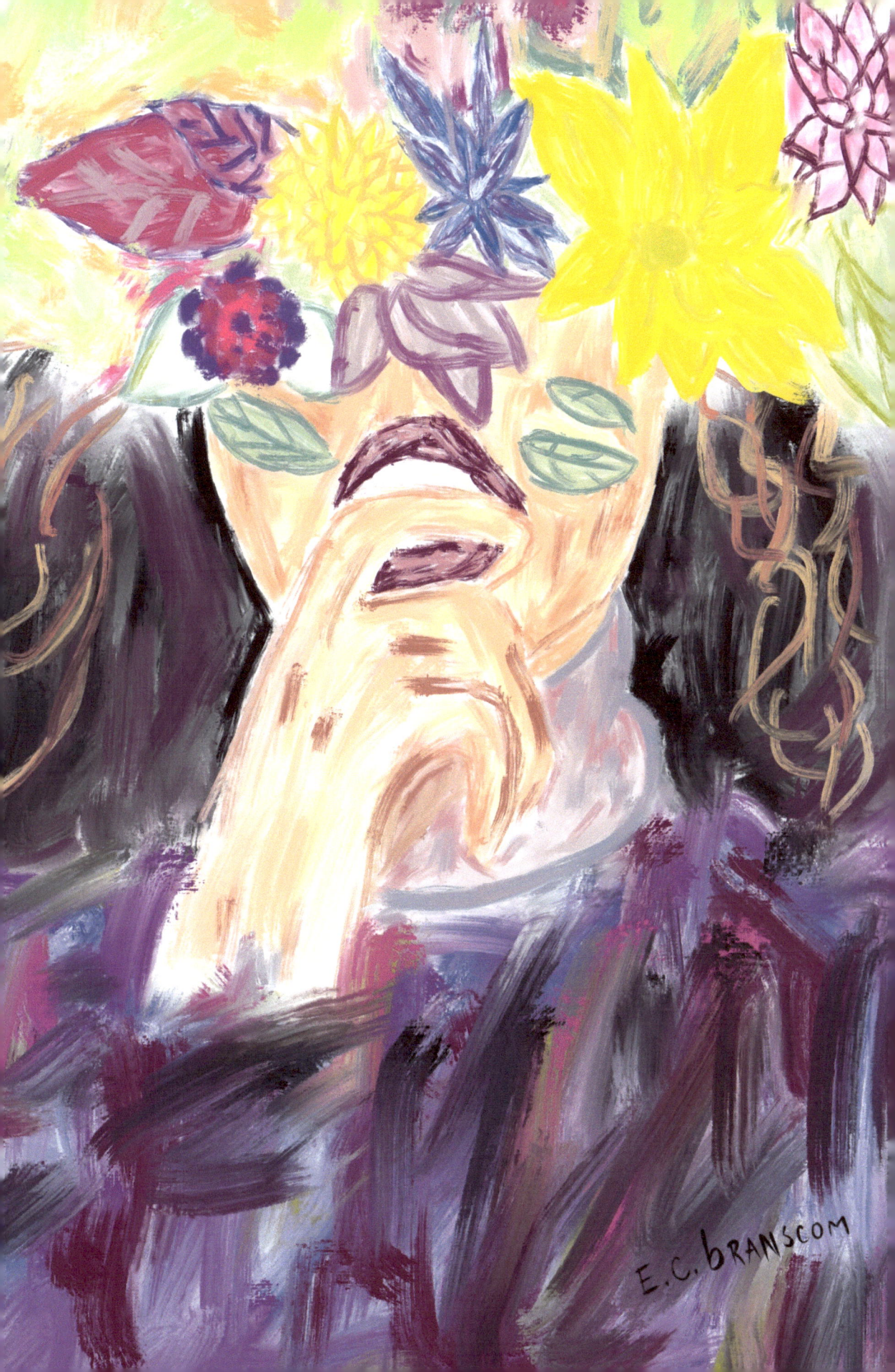

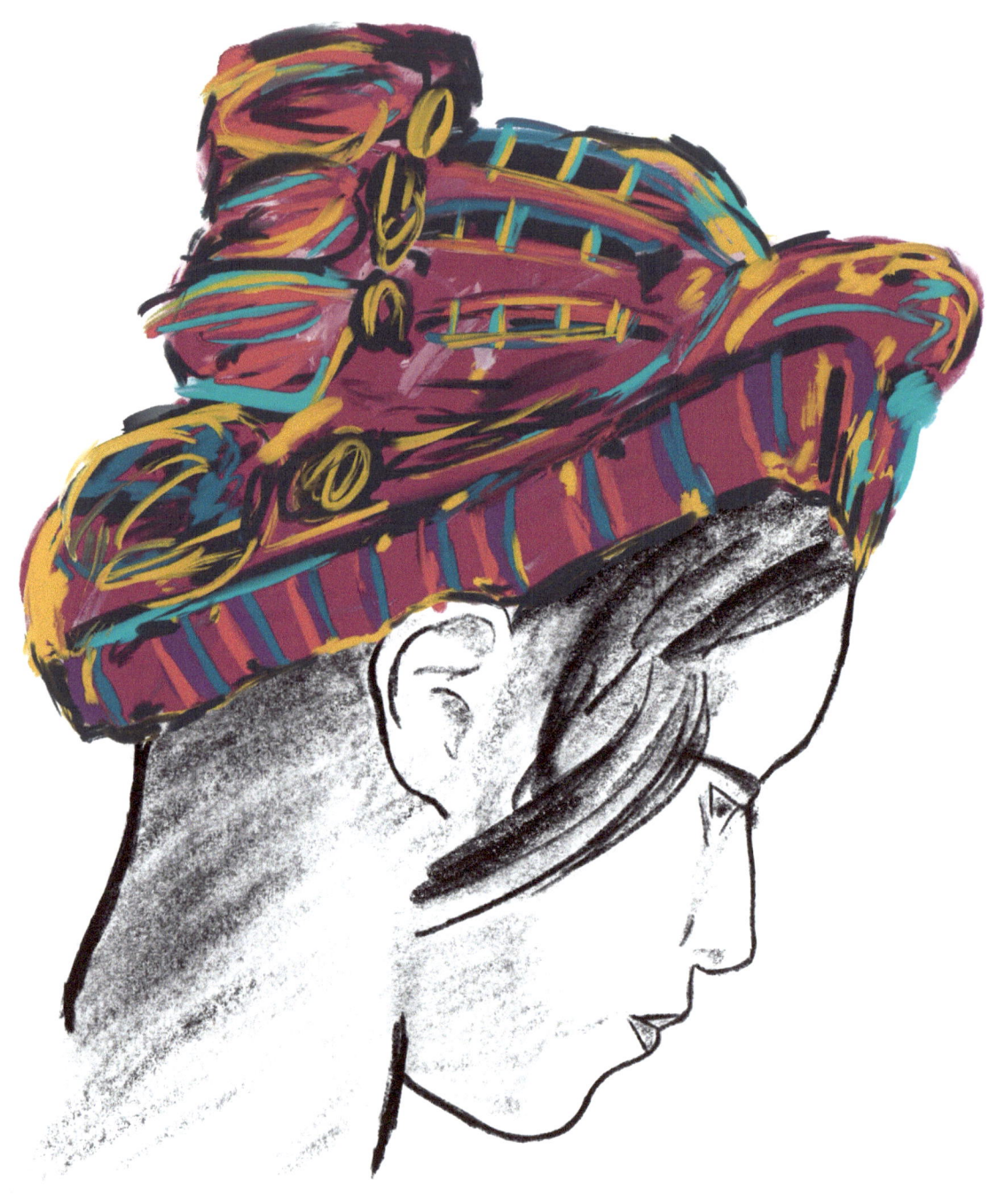

- The Mayan Girl -

Digital portrait.

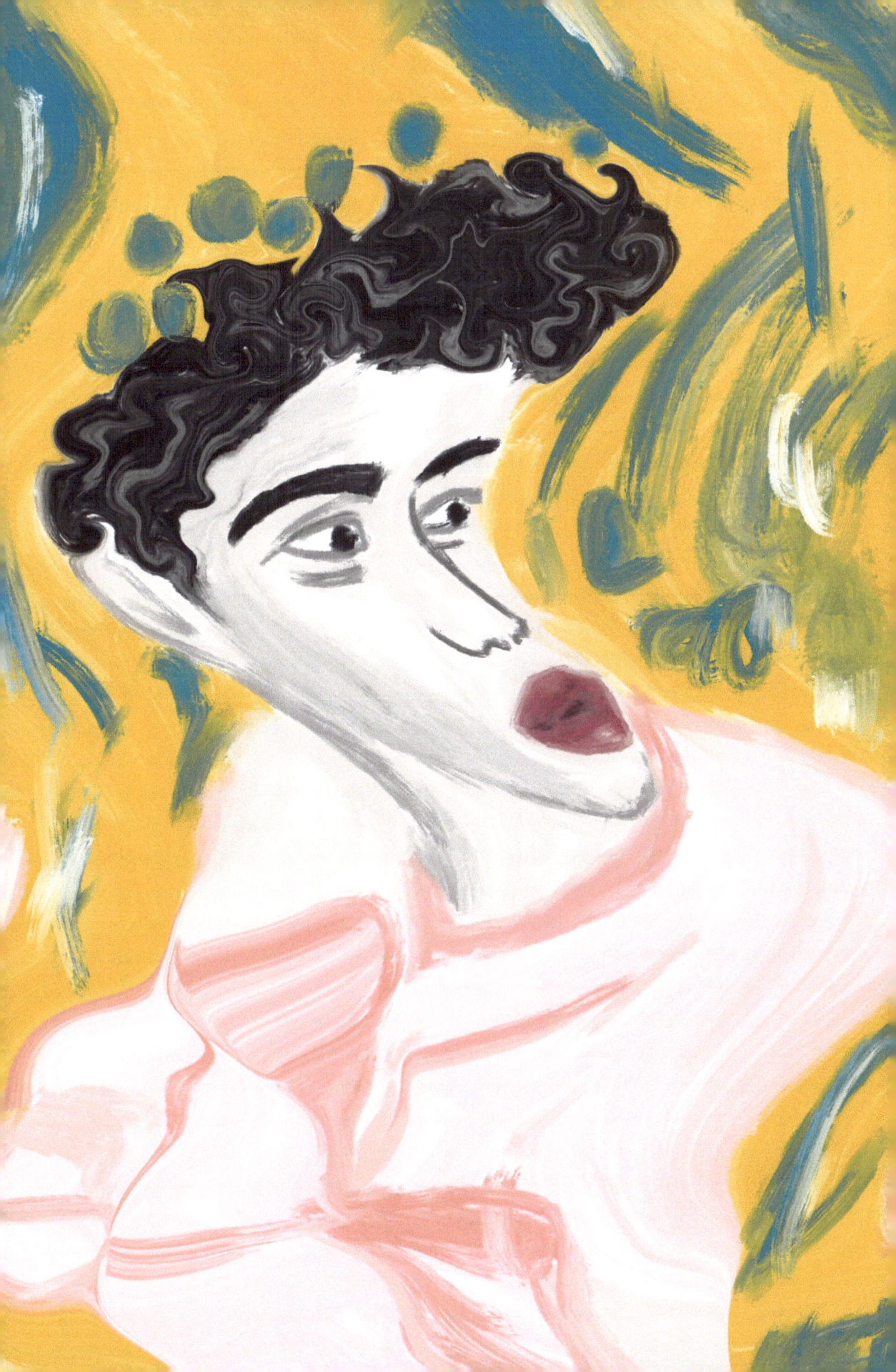

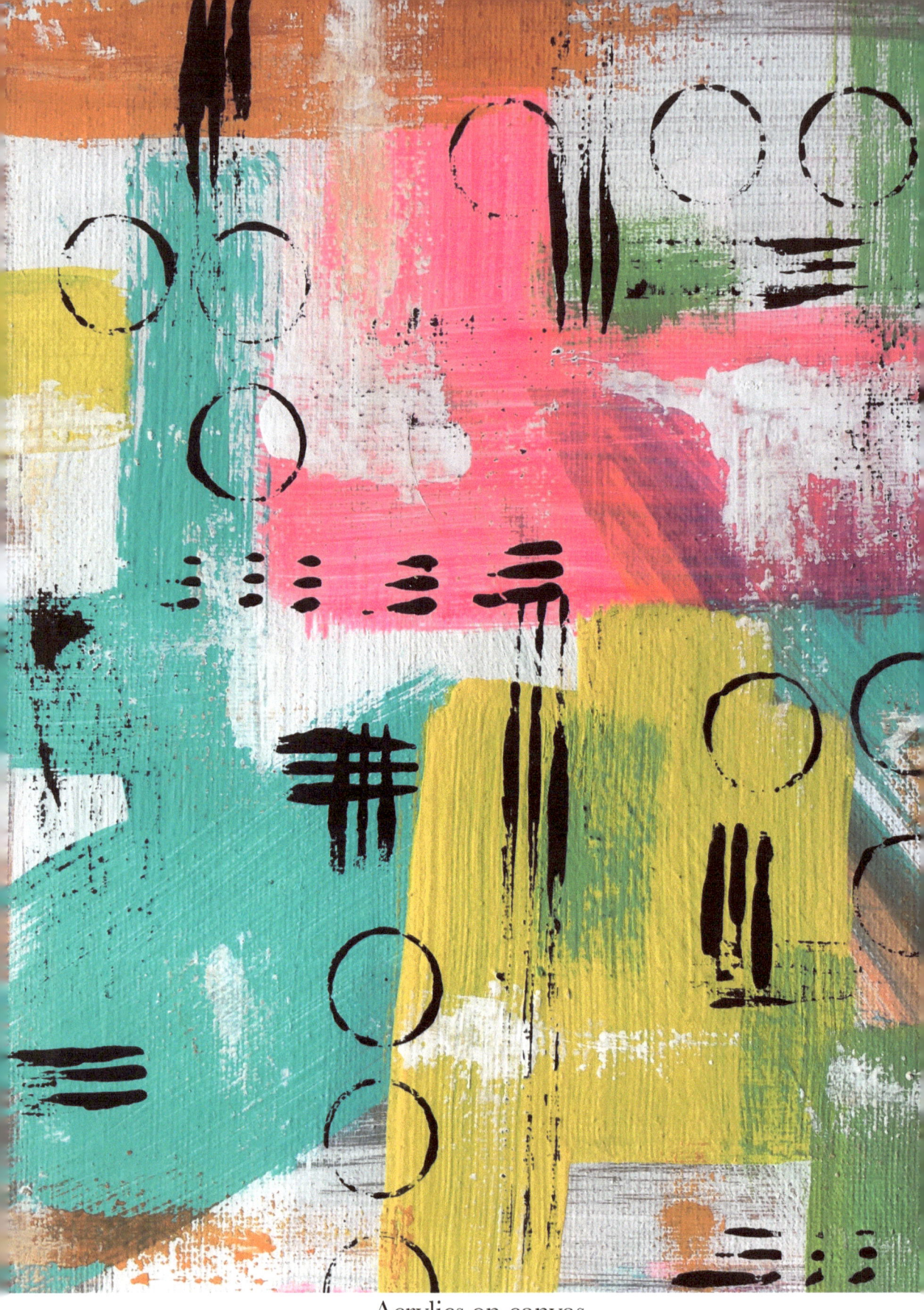

Acrylics on canvas

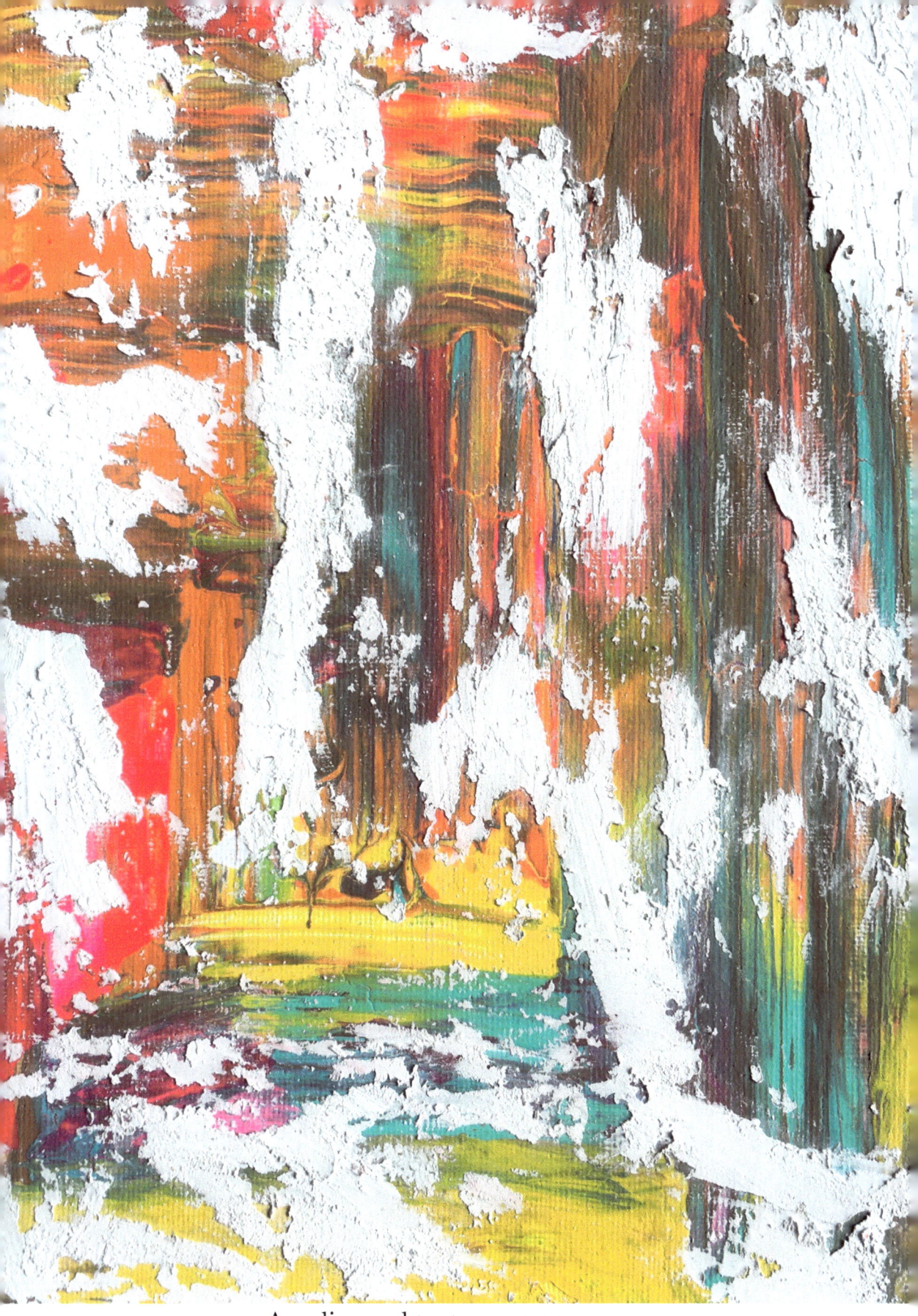
Acrylics and texture on canvas

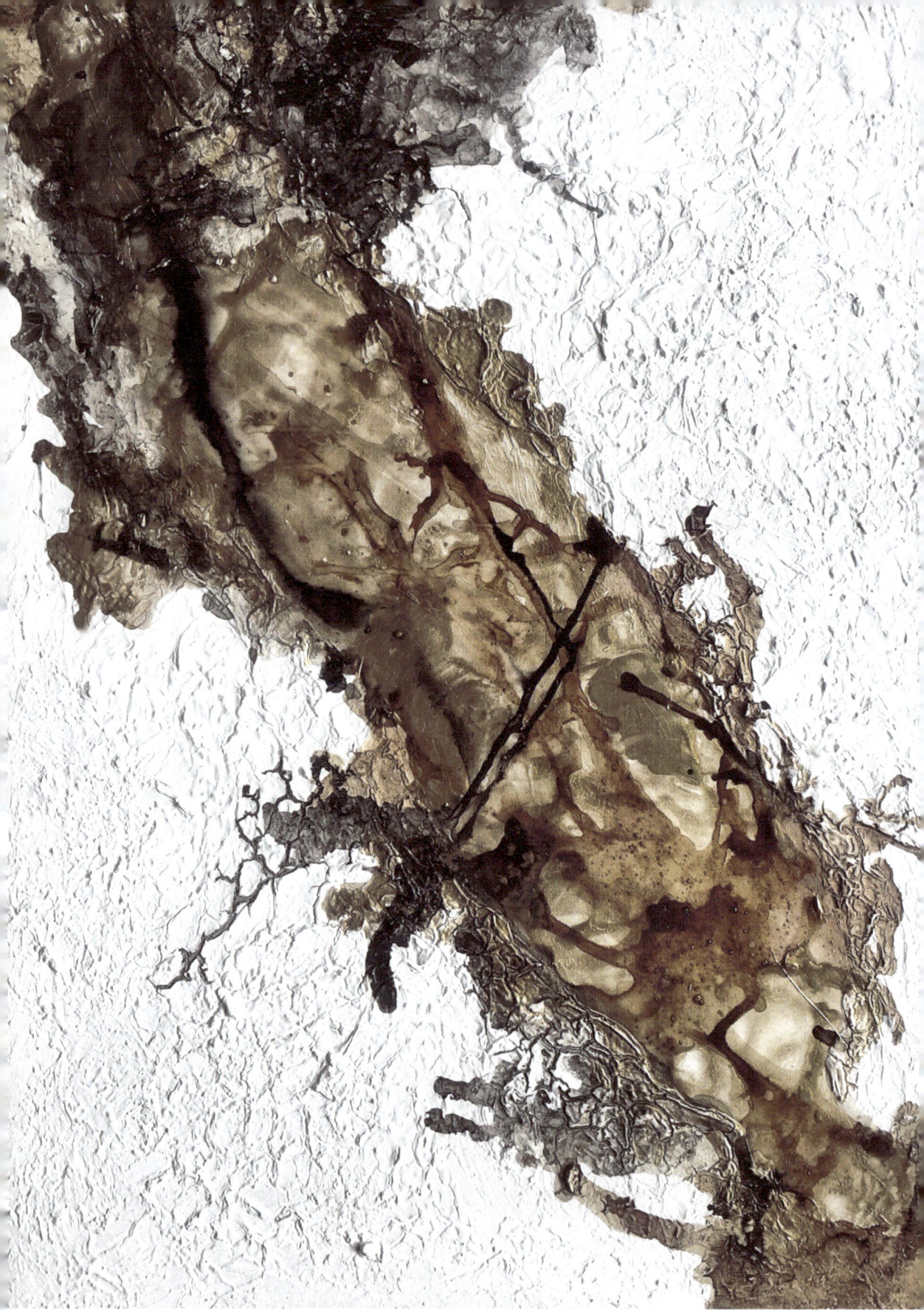

Acrylics and texture on canvas

Golden acrylics, drawing ink, texture, coffee painting.

Acrylics on canvas

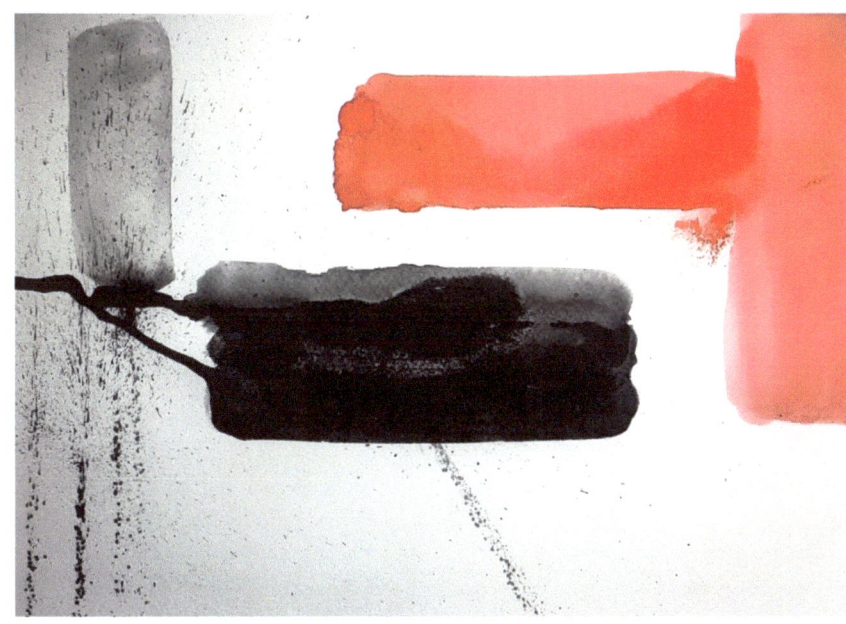

Chinese ink

Acrylics

Acrylics on canvas

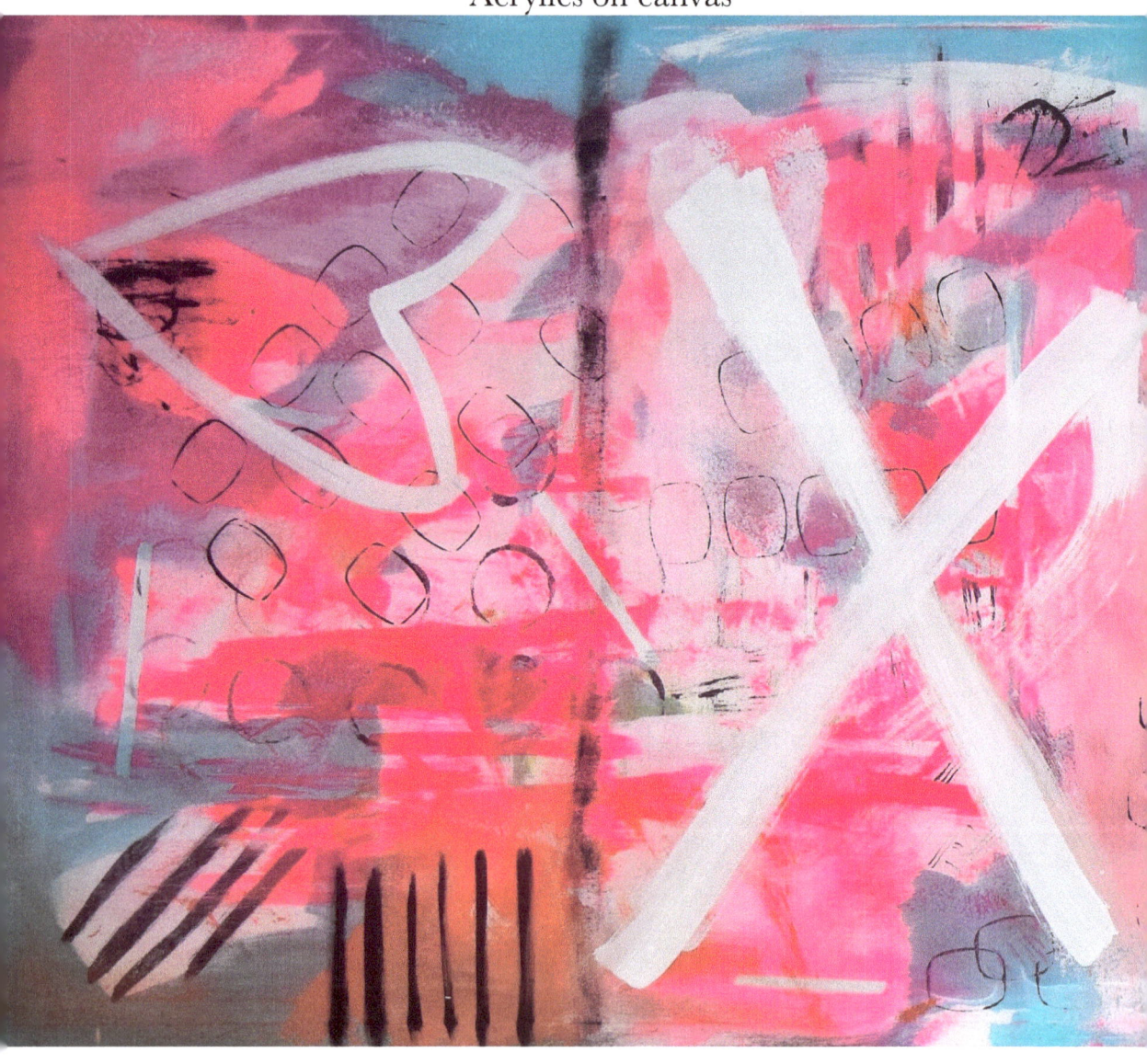

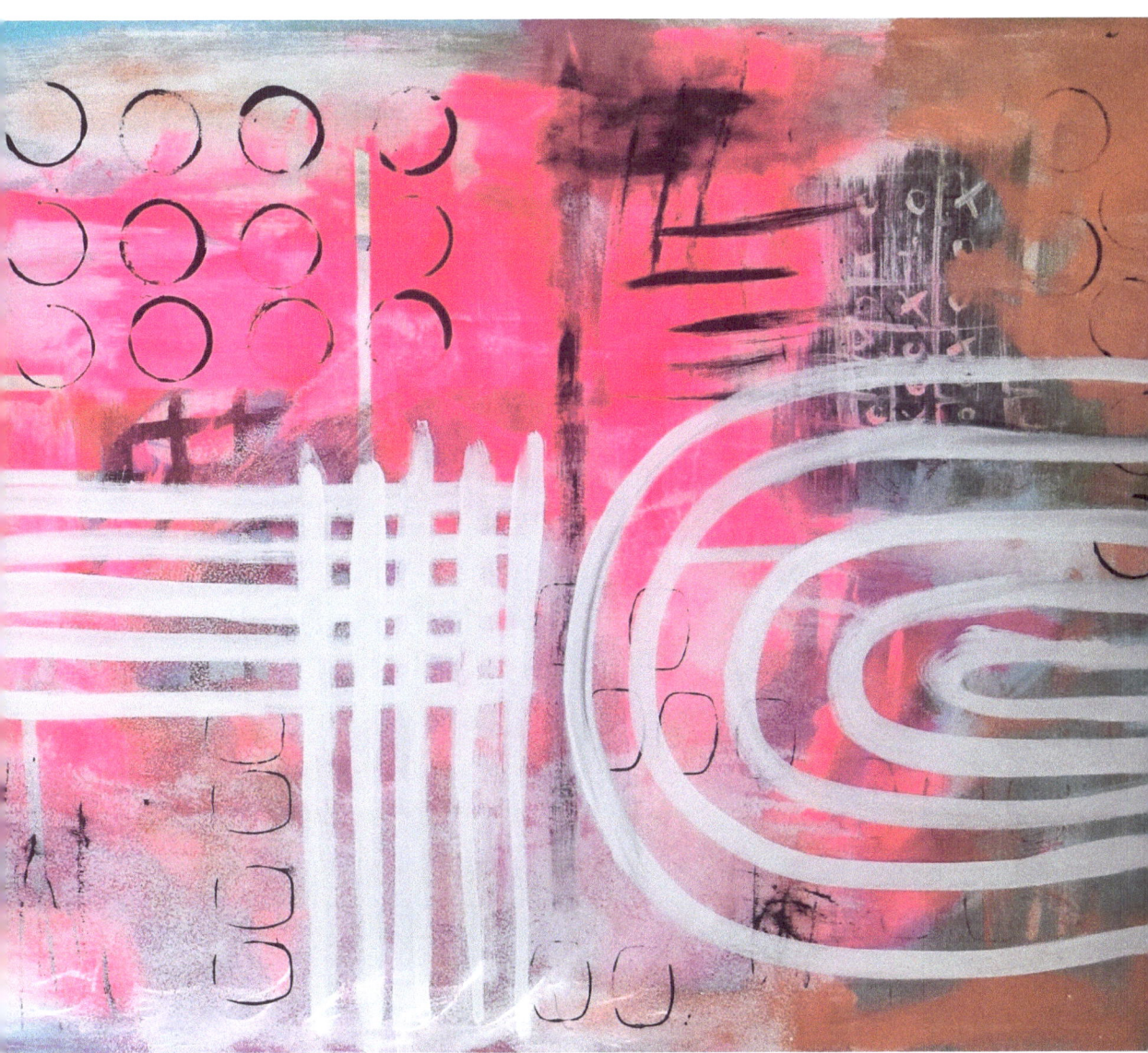

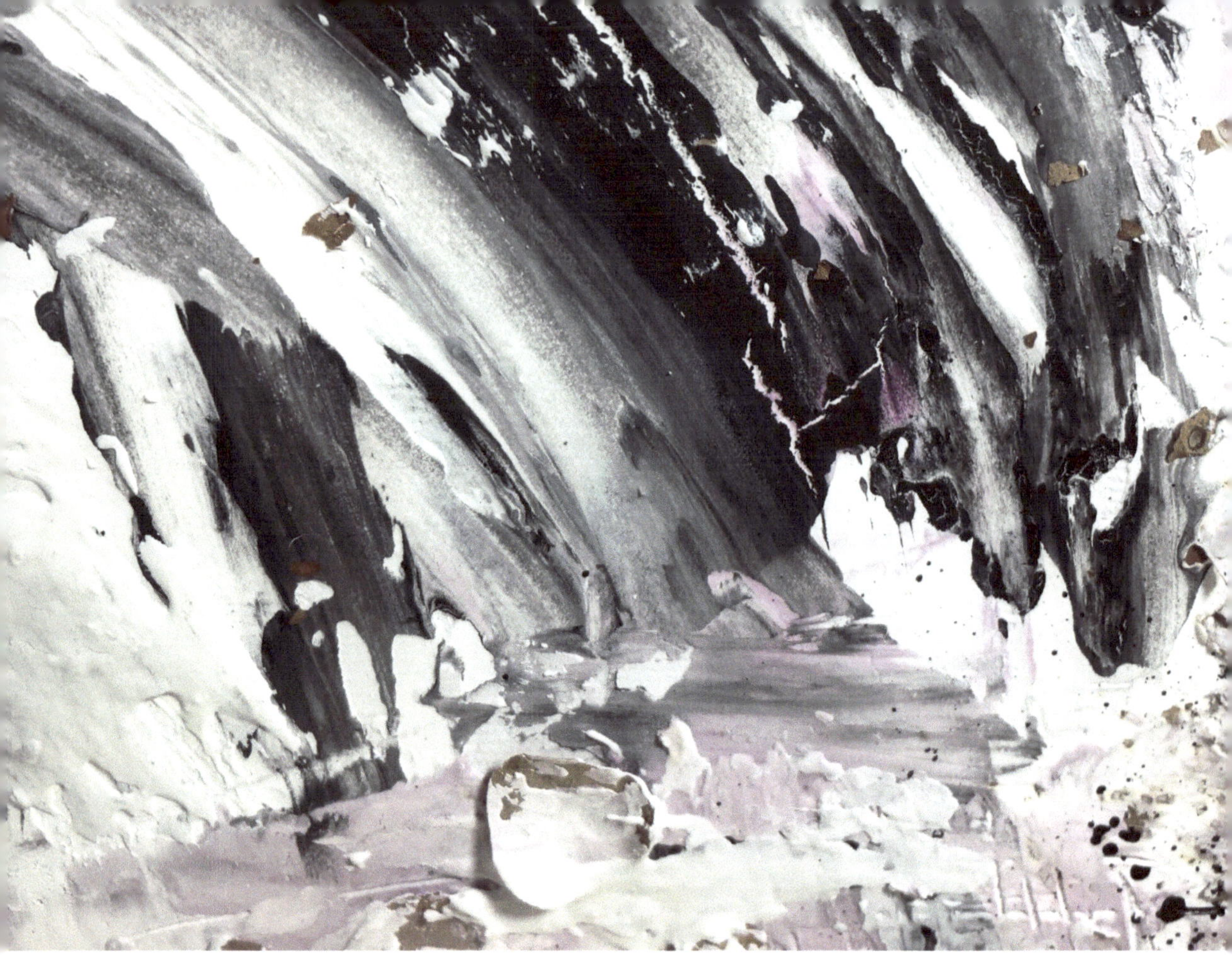

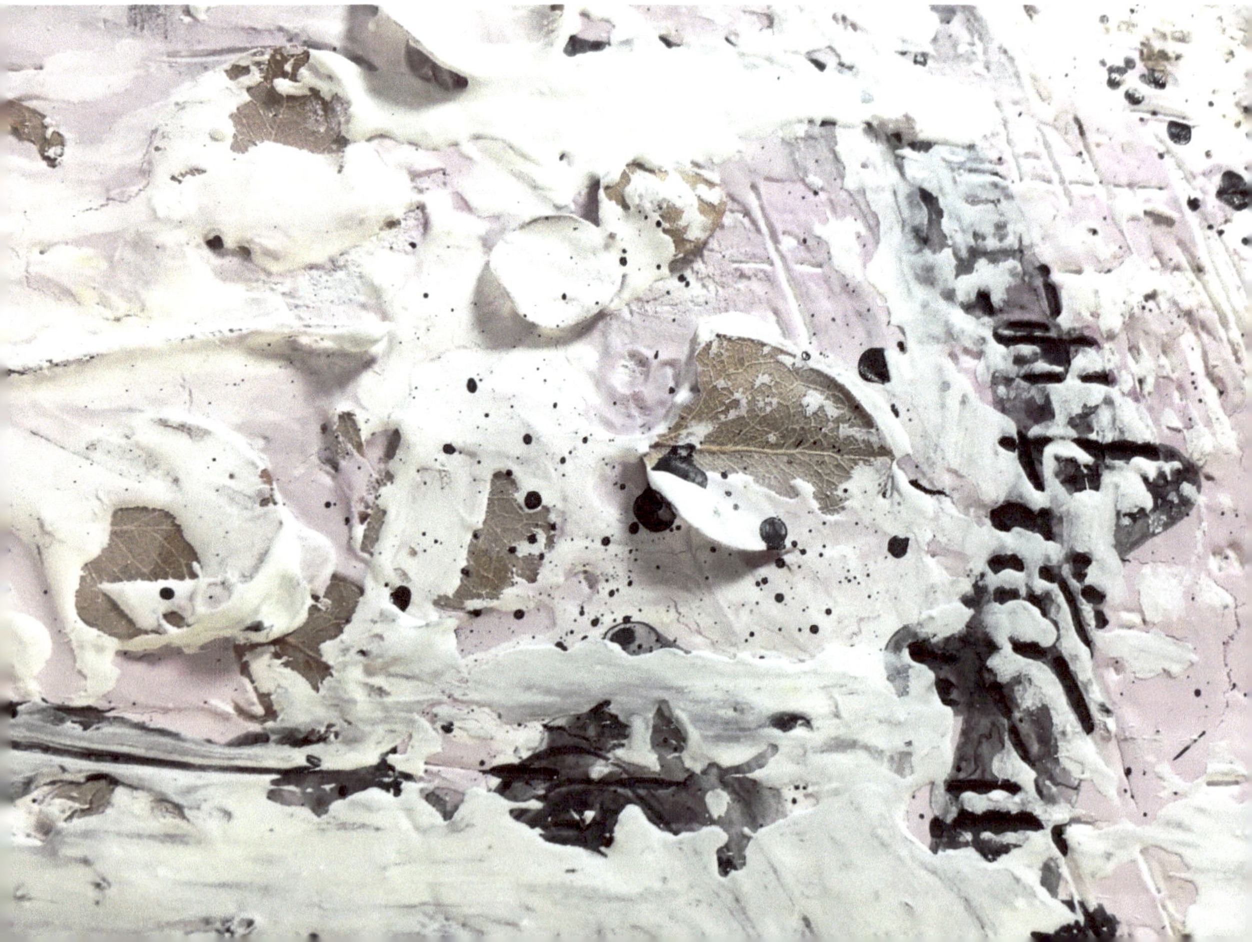

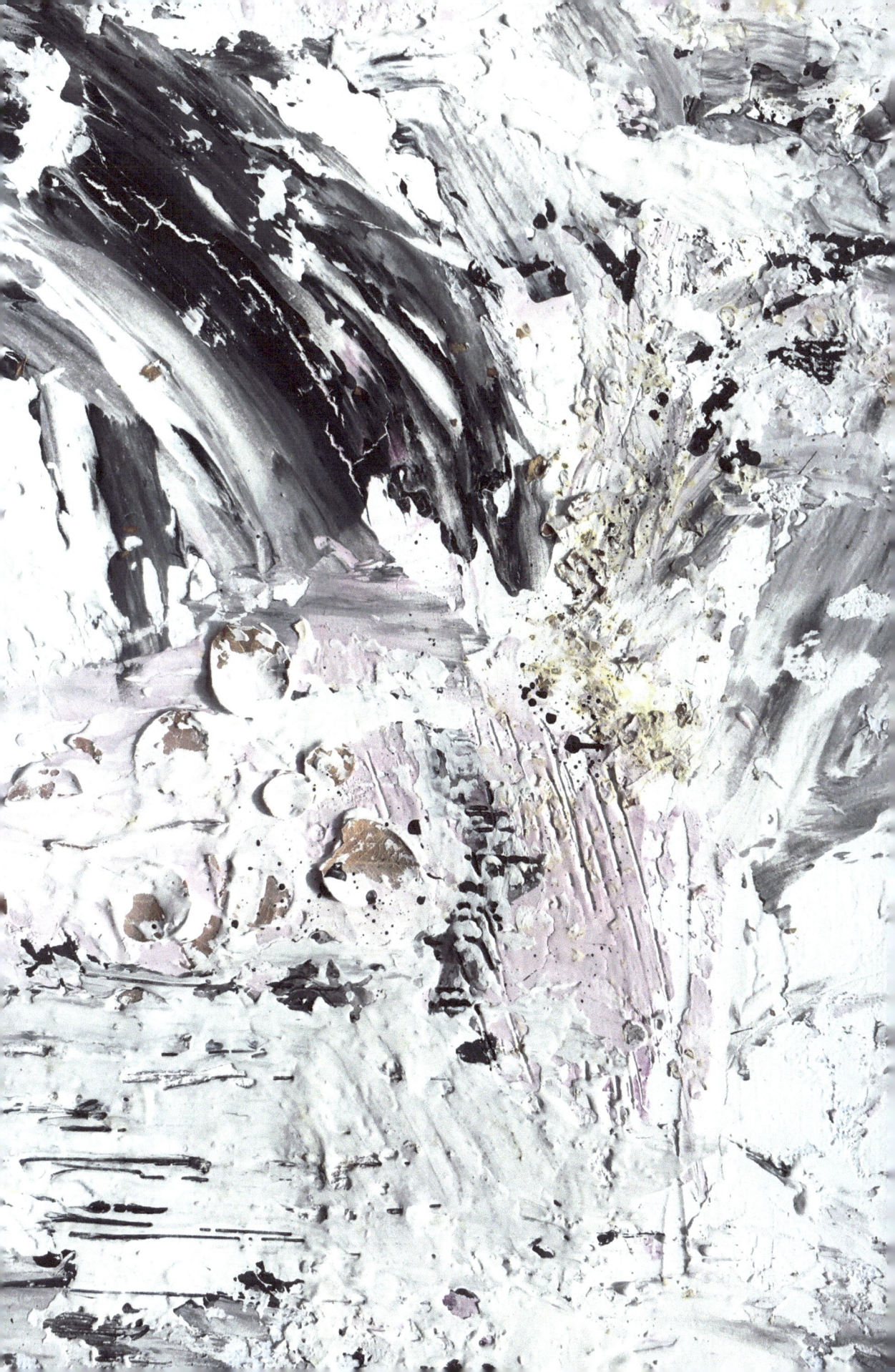

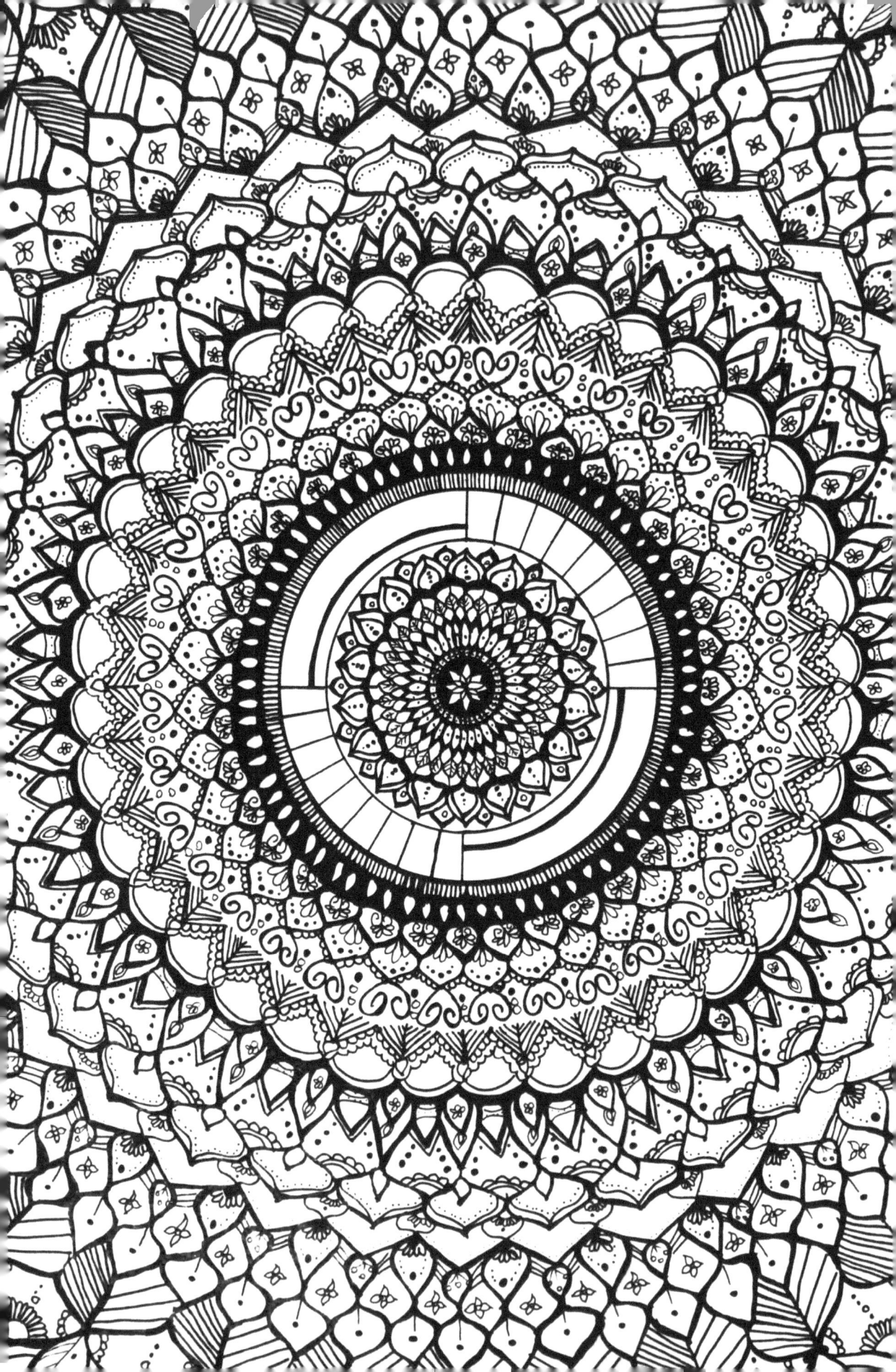

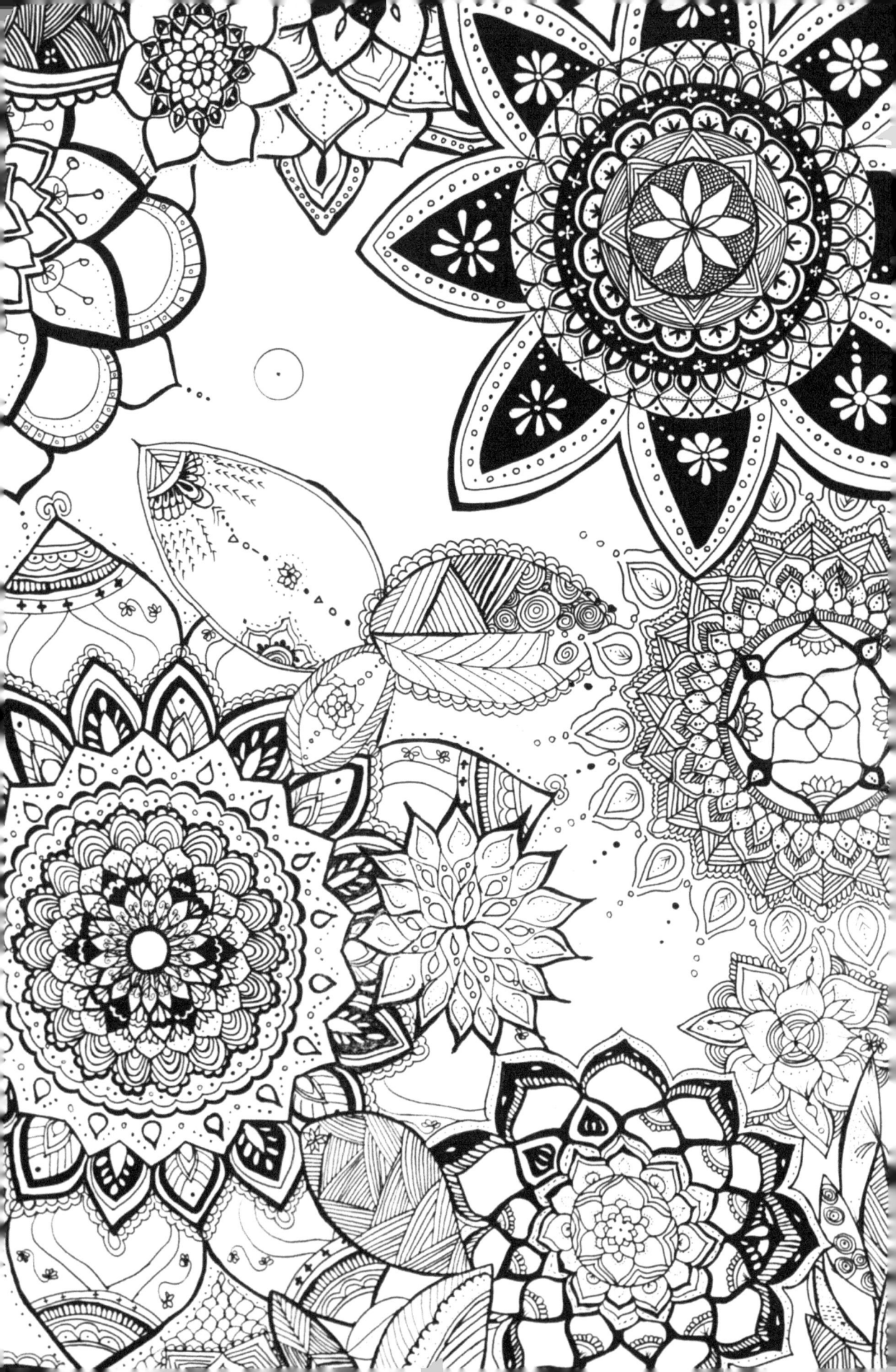

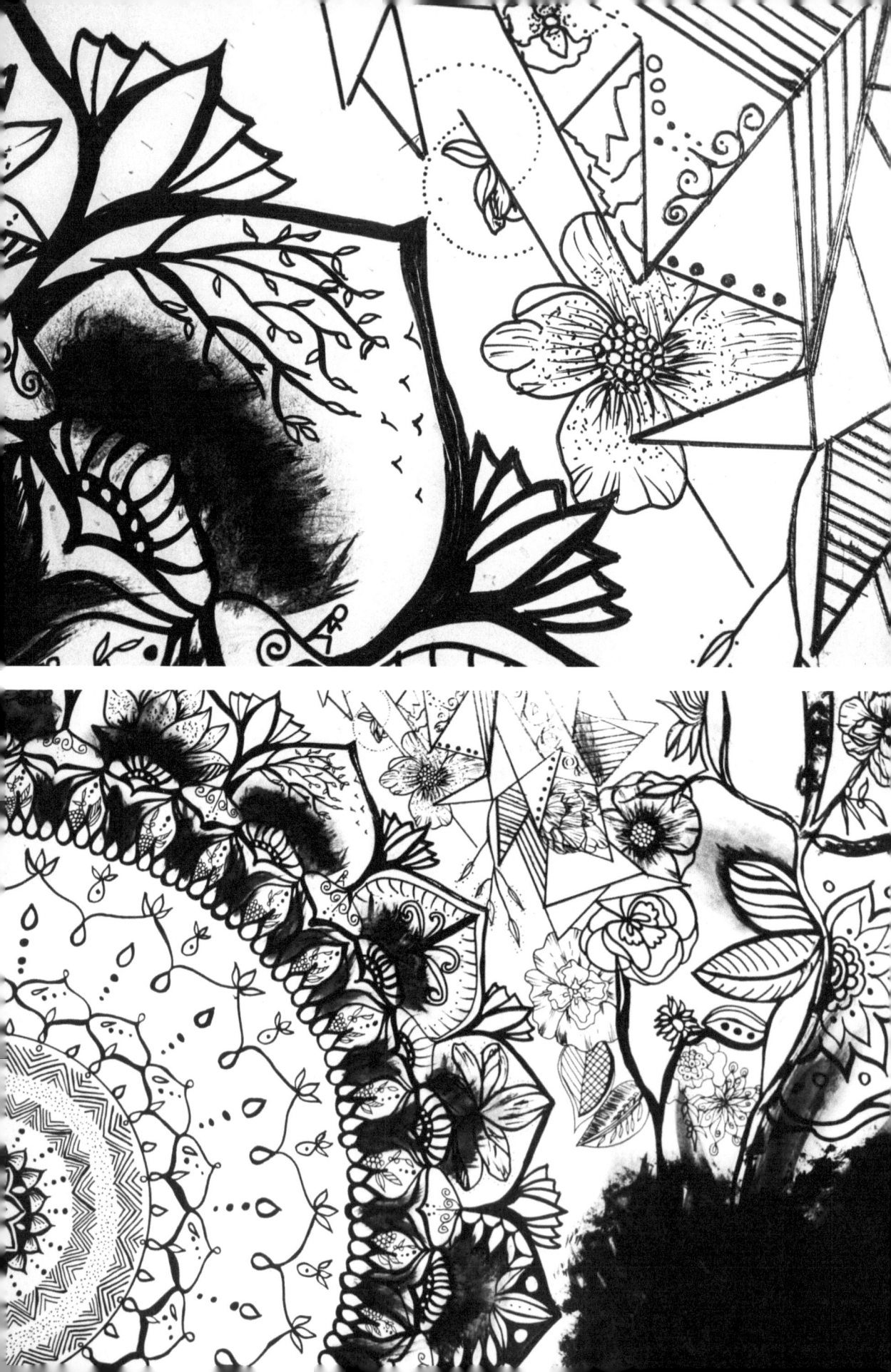

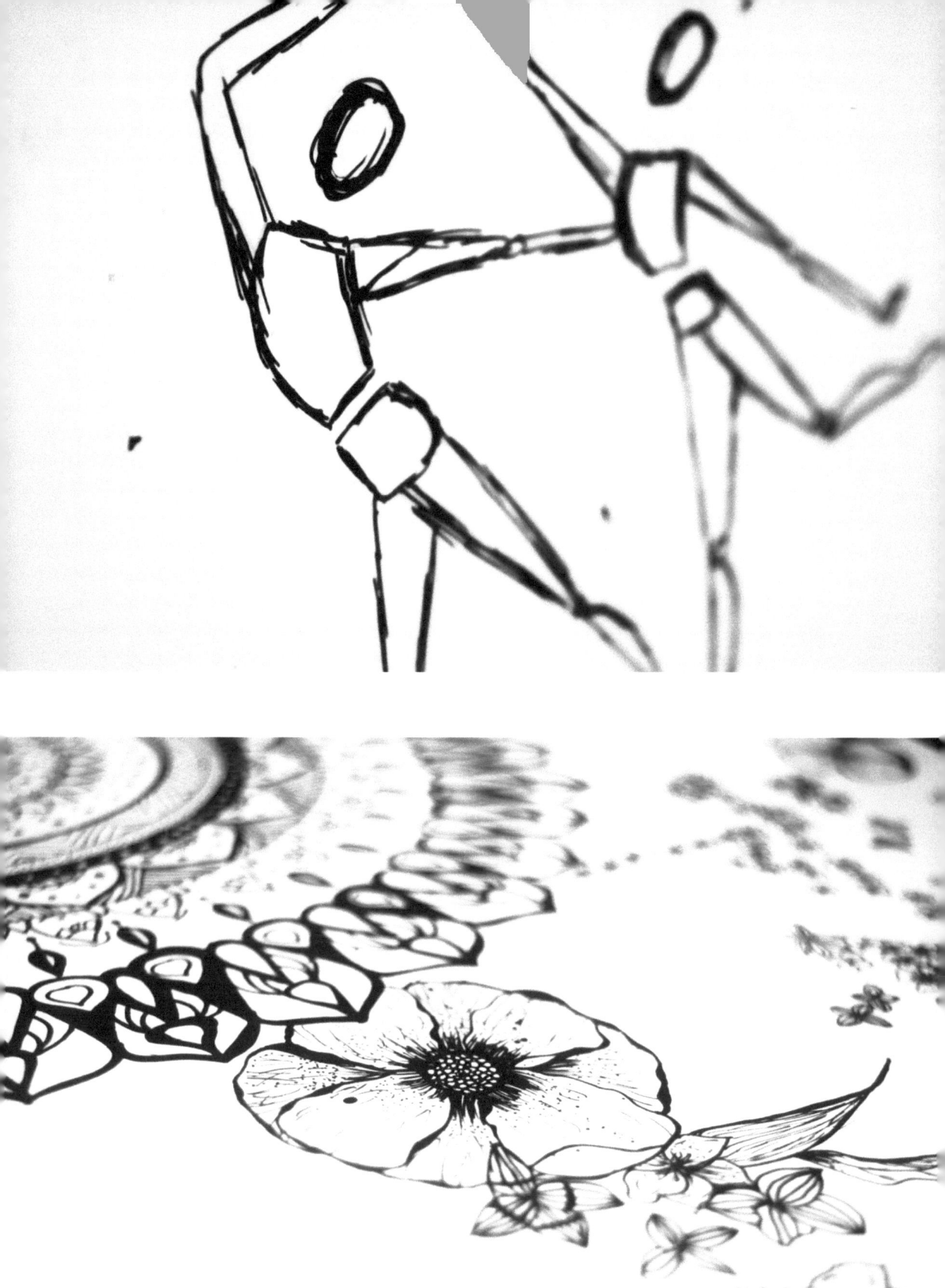

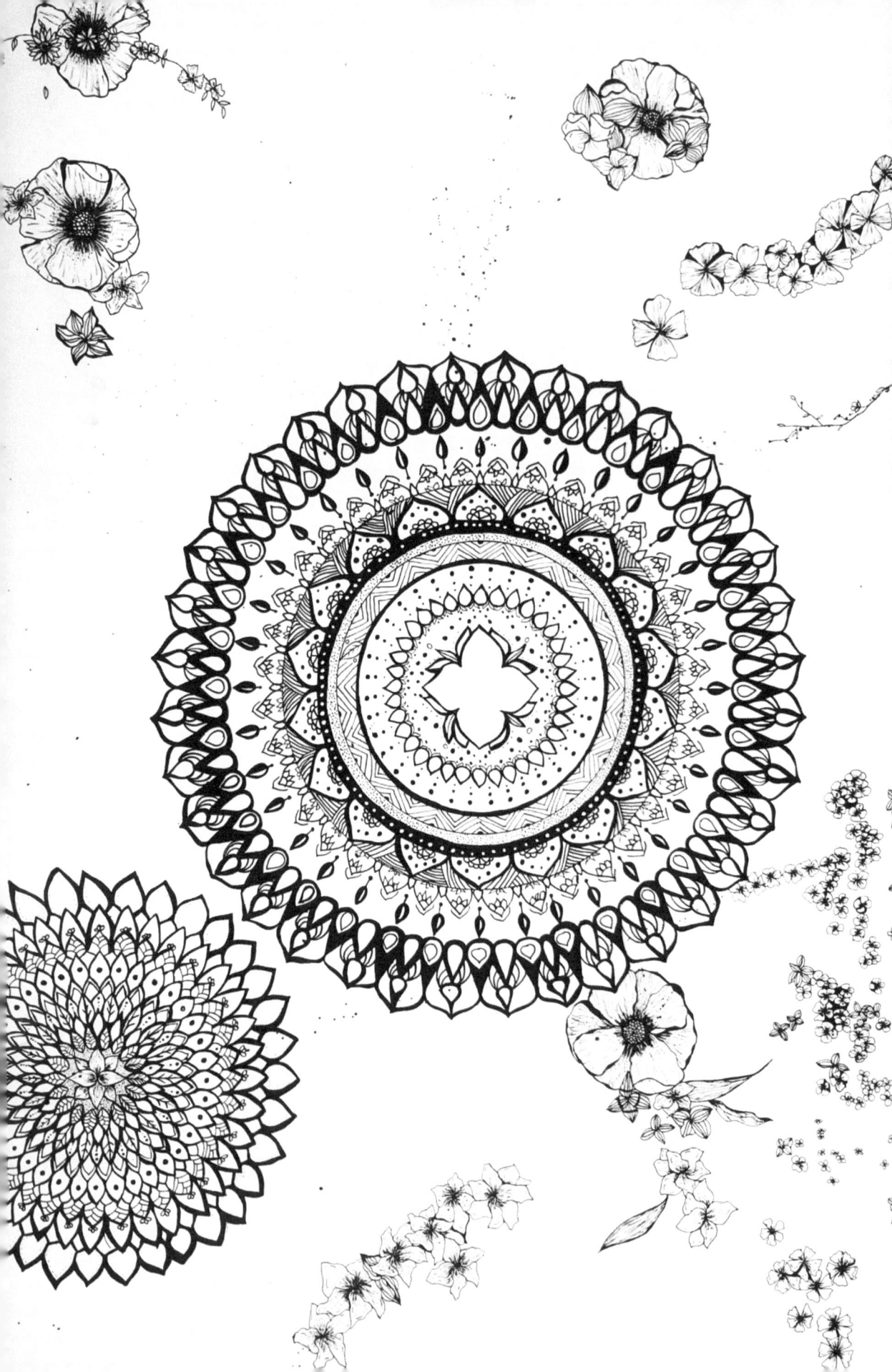

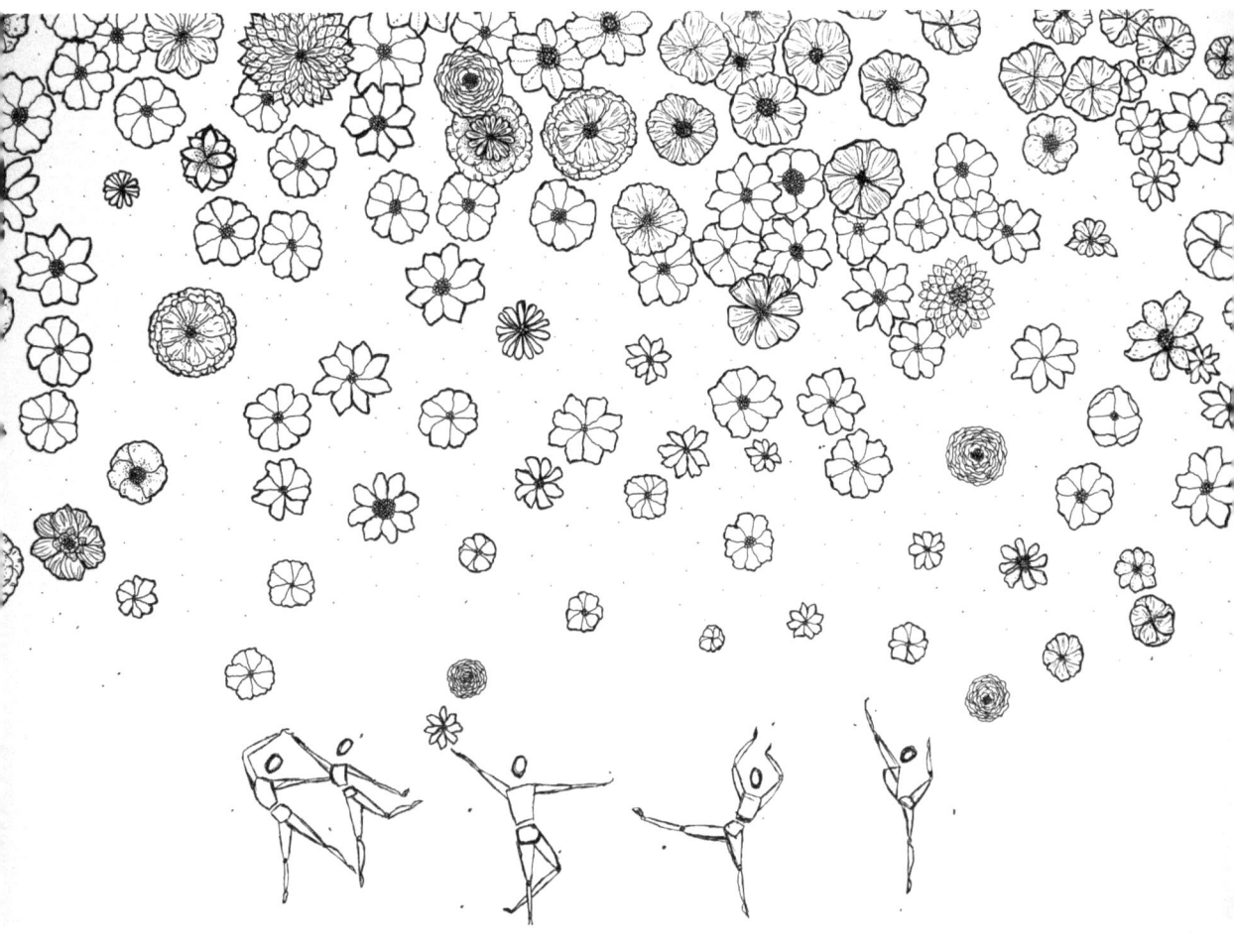

"Dance in the Storm"

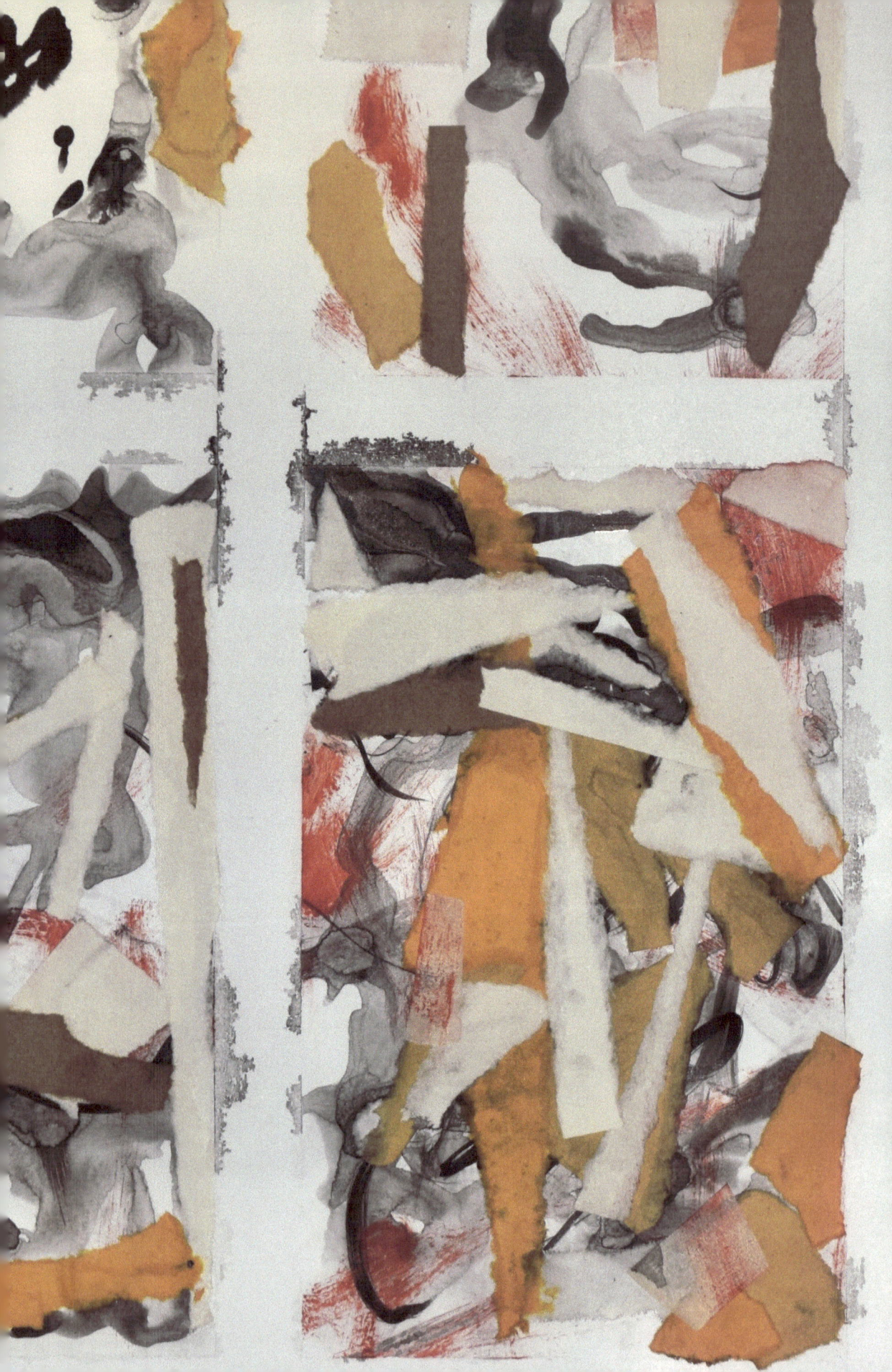

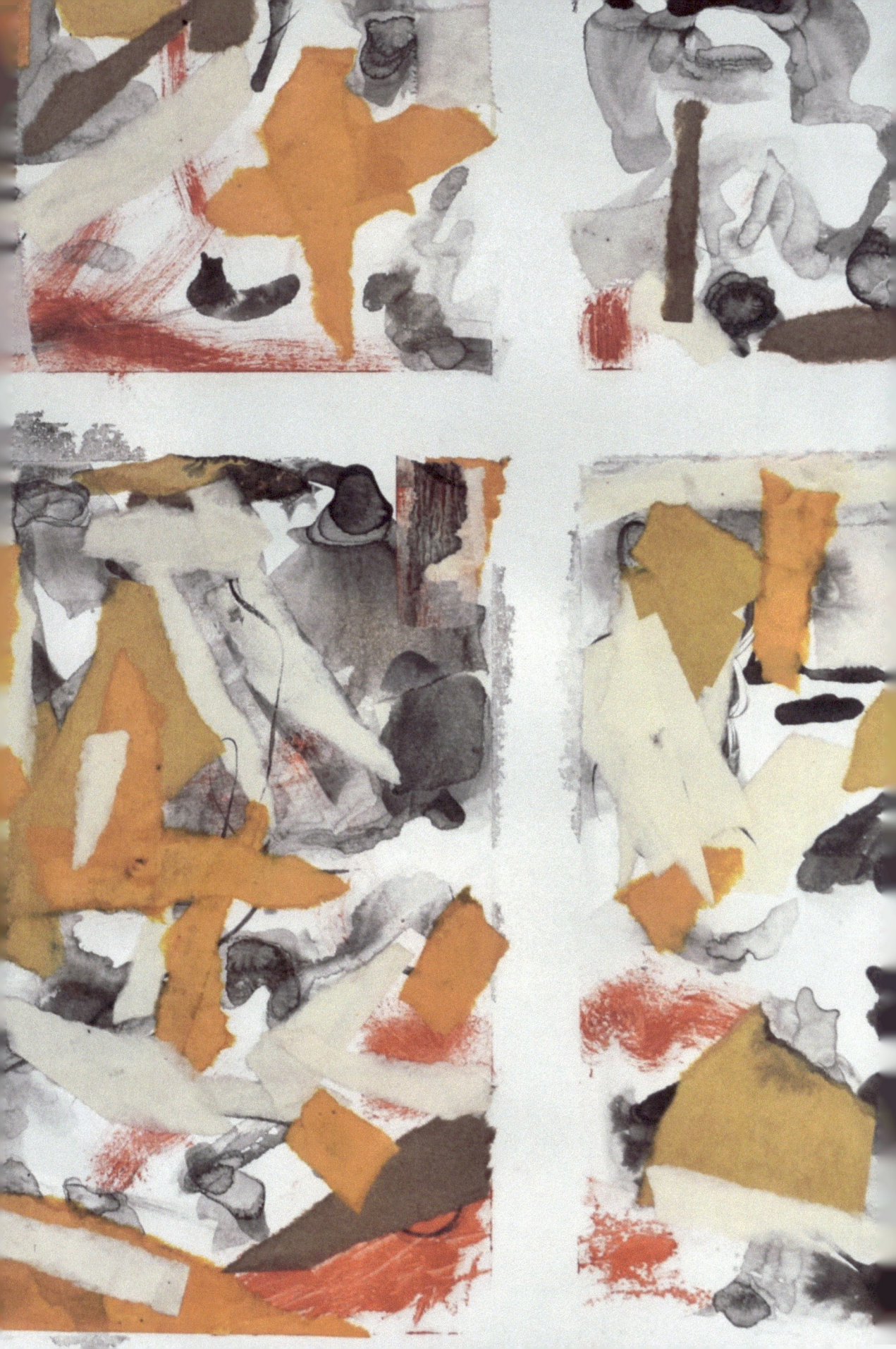

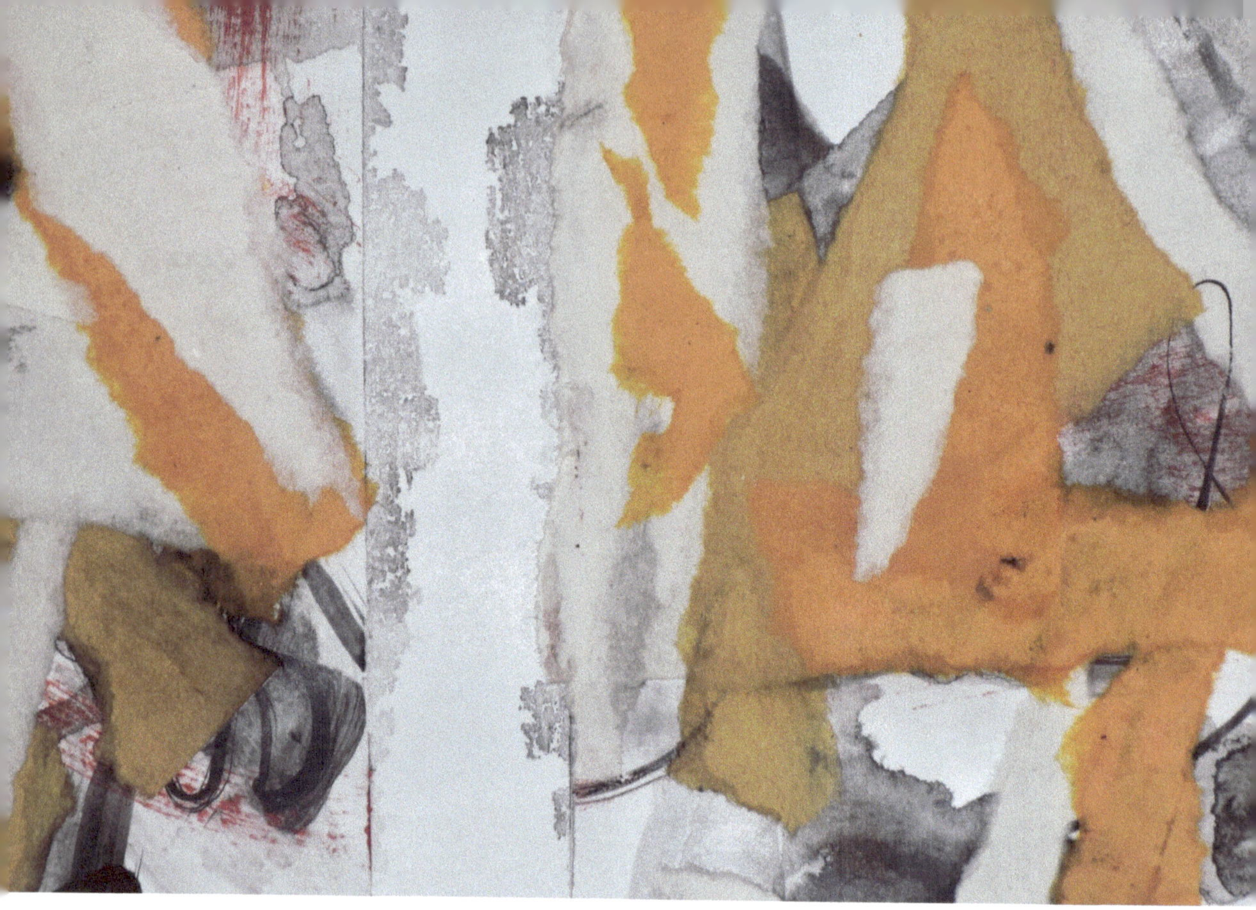

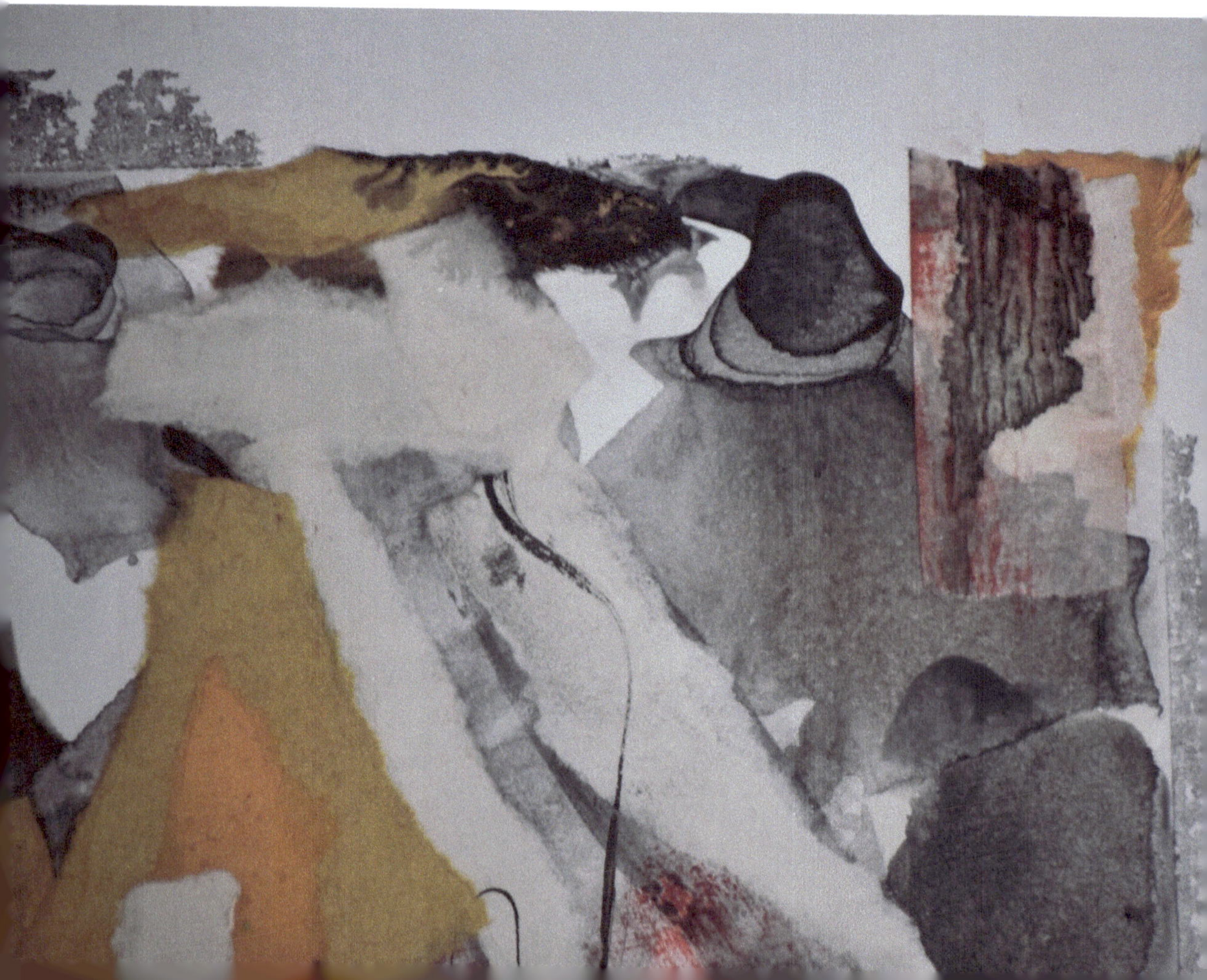

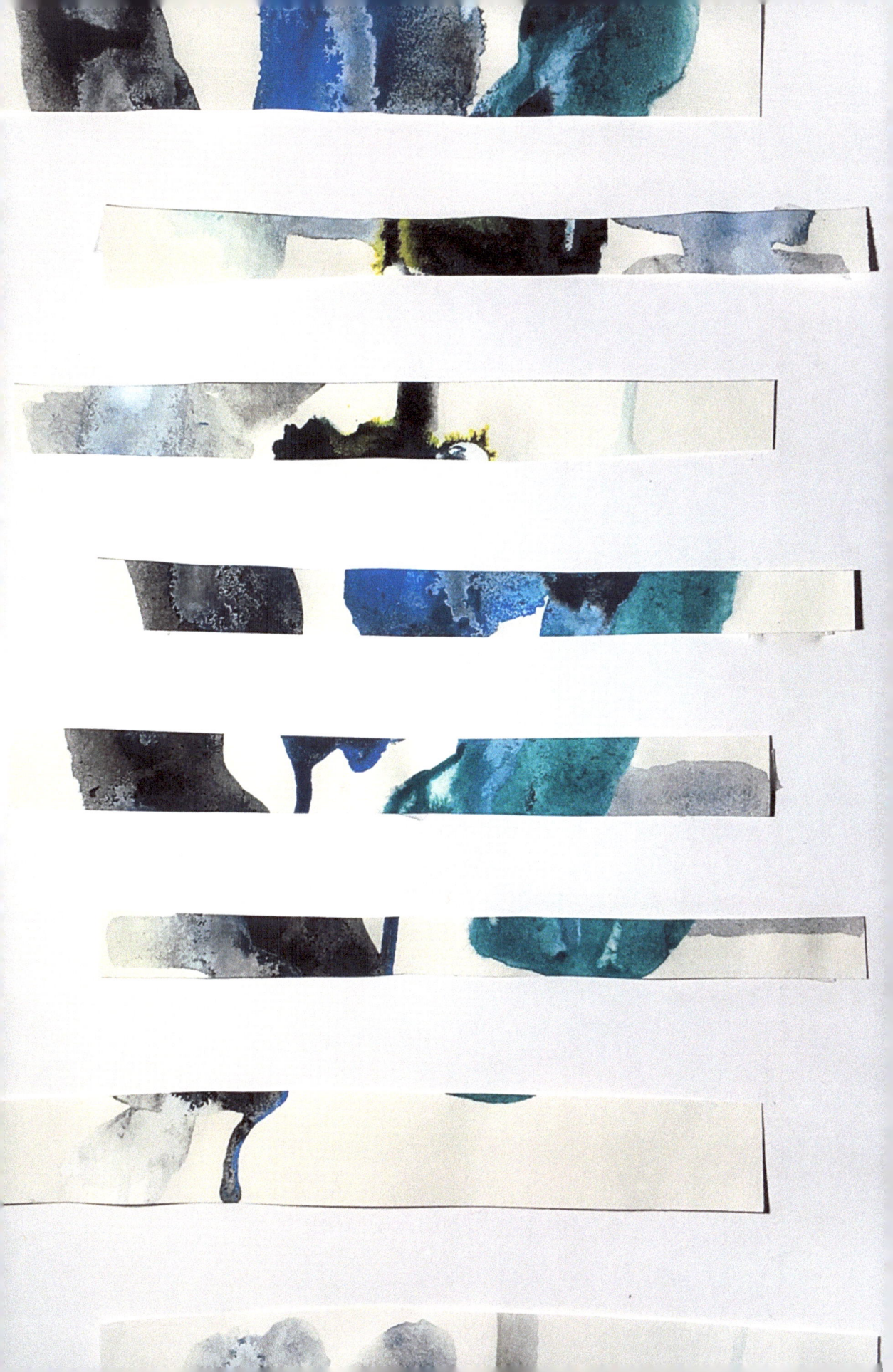

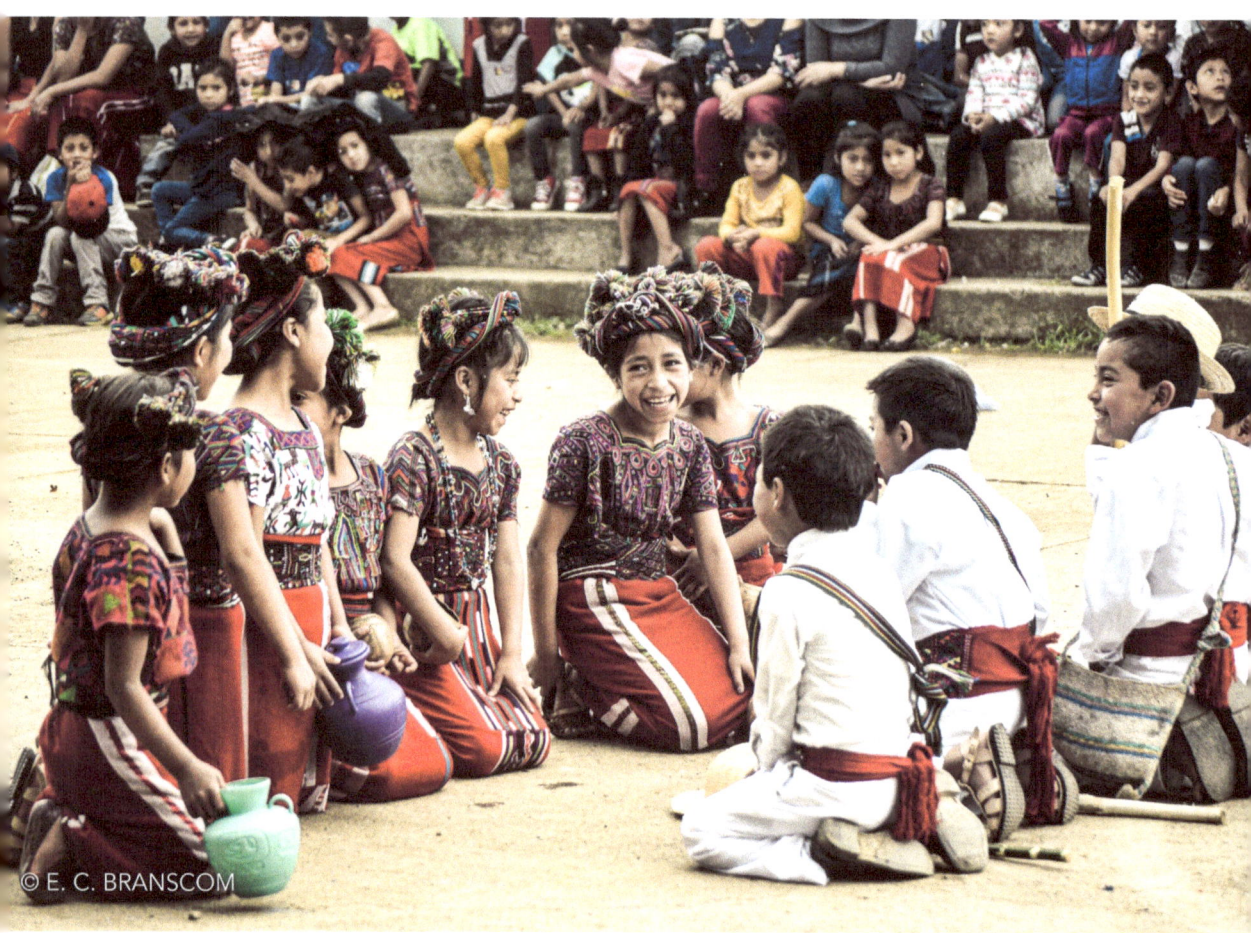

"The meet"
Guatemala 2,018

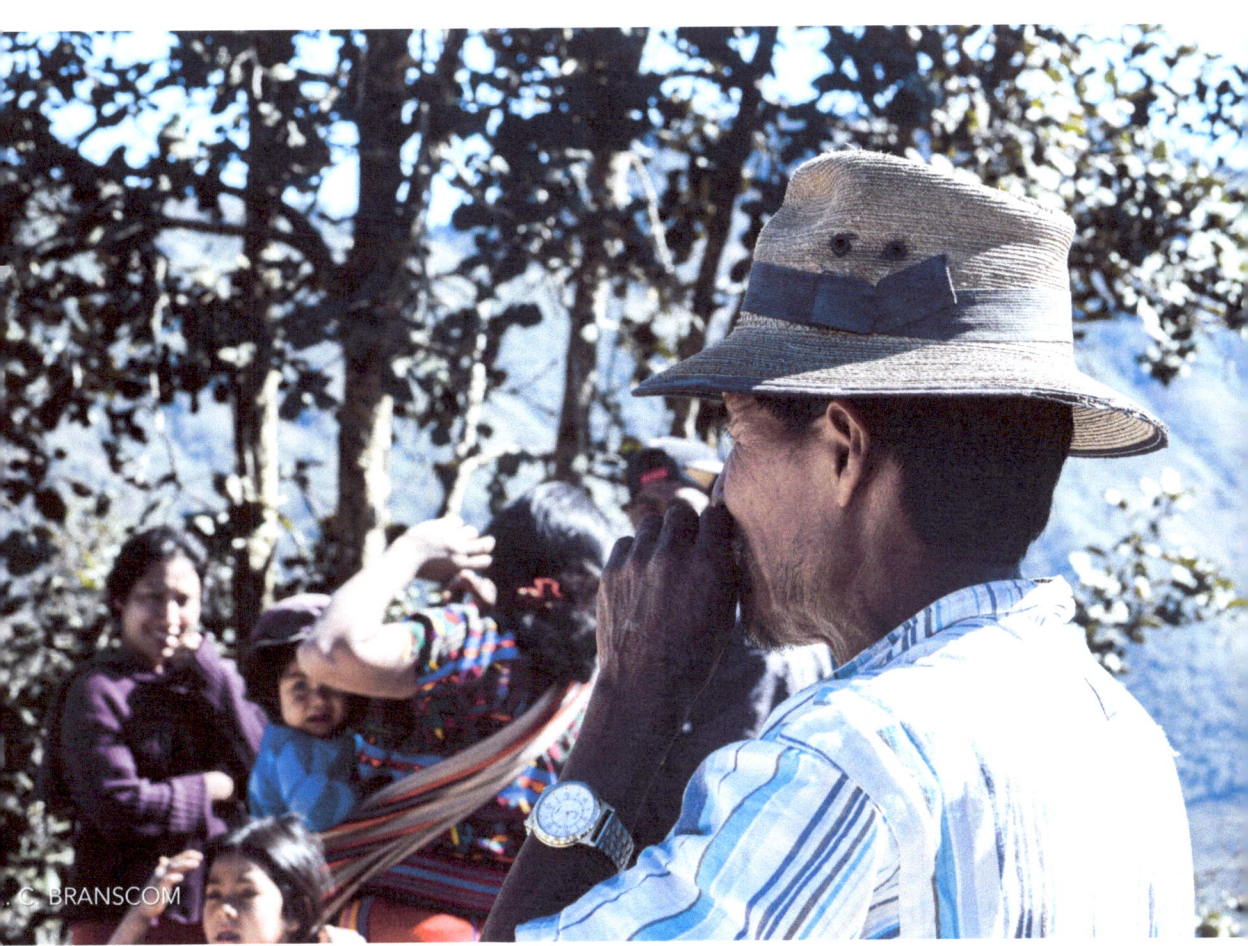

"The man and the hat"
Guatemala 2,018

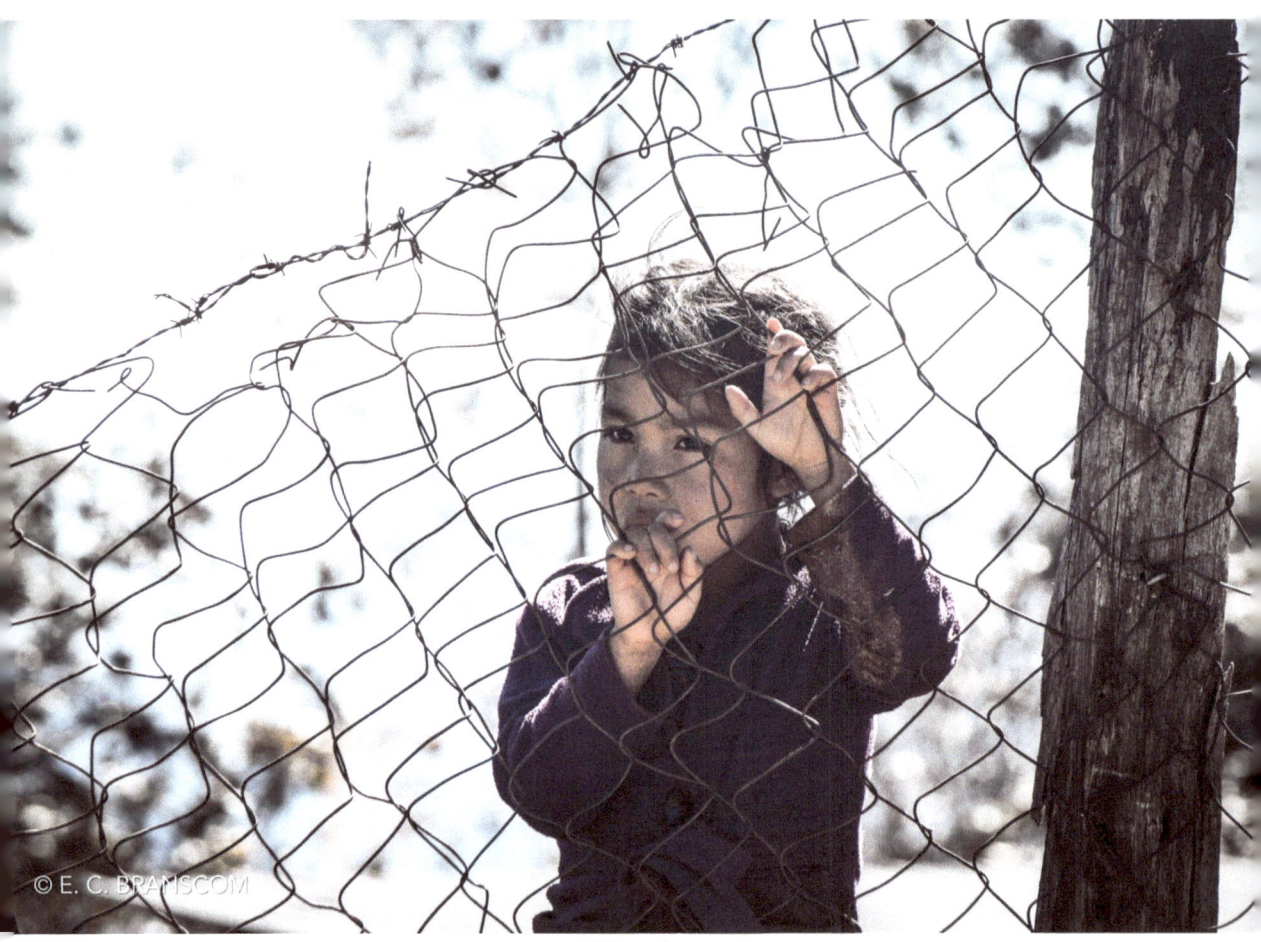

"The hope"
Guatemala 2,018

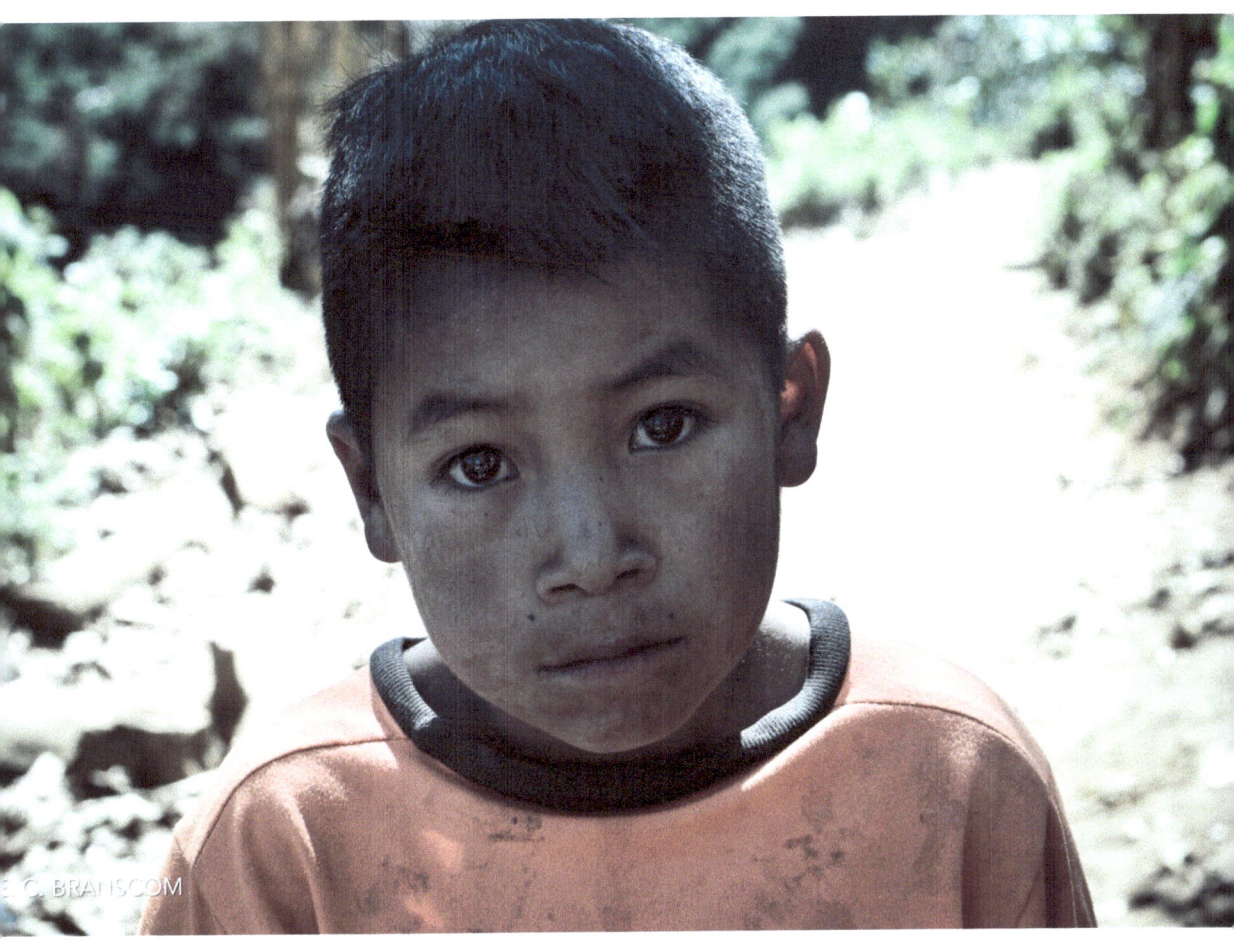

"The kid in orange"
Guatemala 2,018

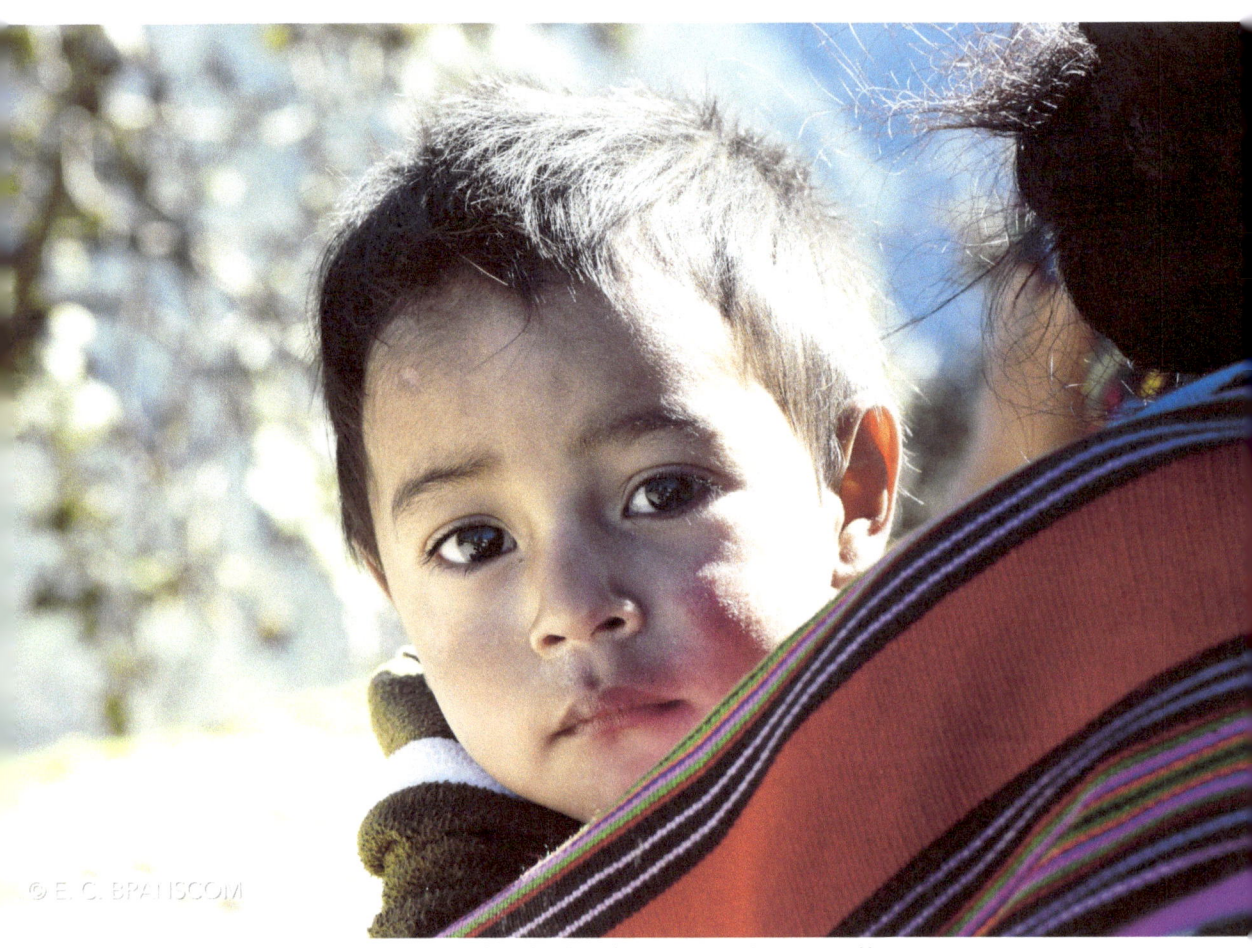

"The baby in mama's arms"
Guatemala 2,018

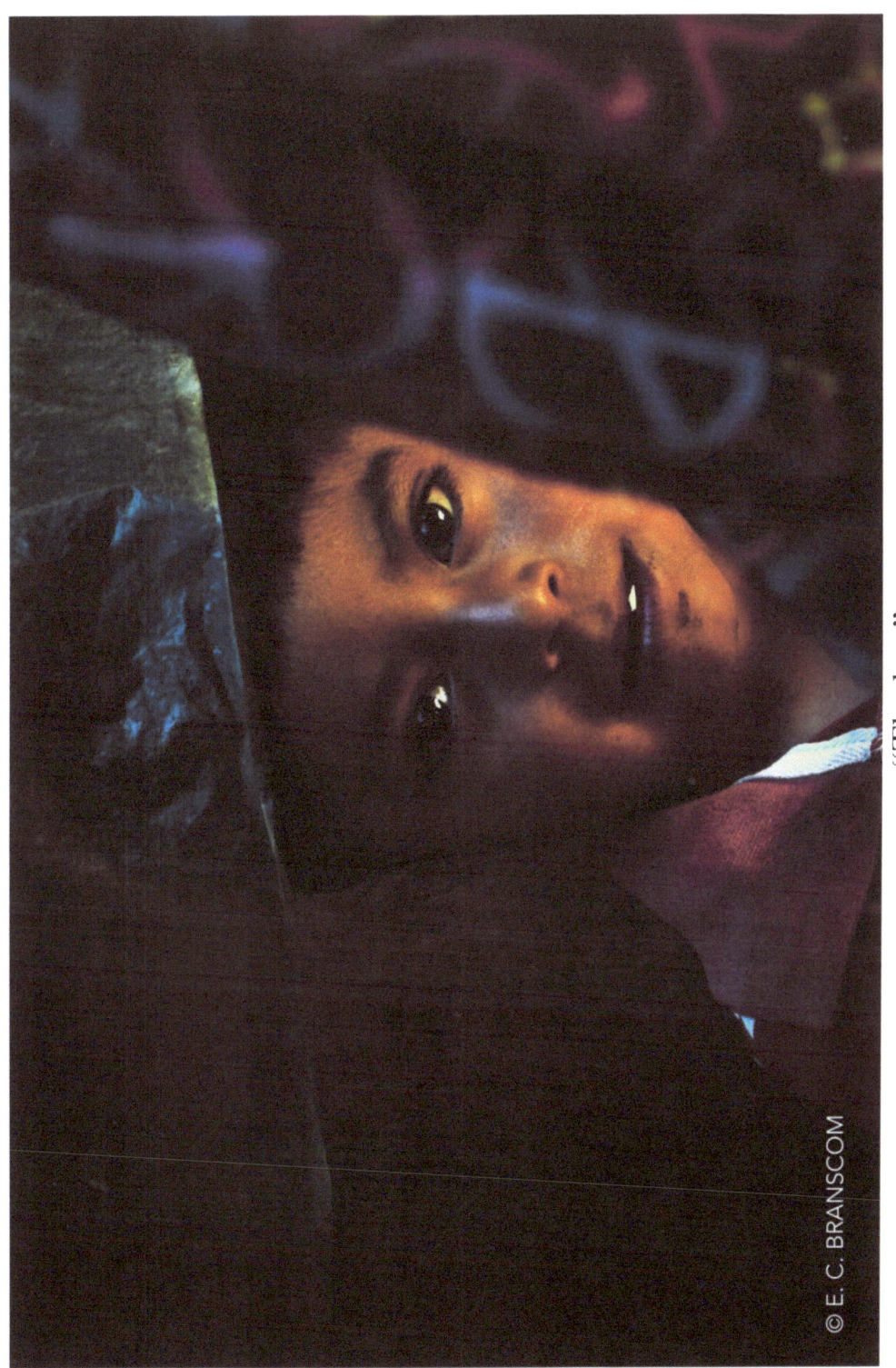

"The boy"
Guatemala 2,018

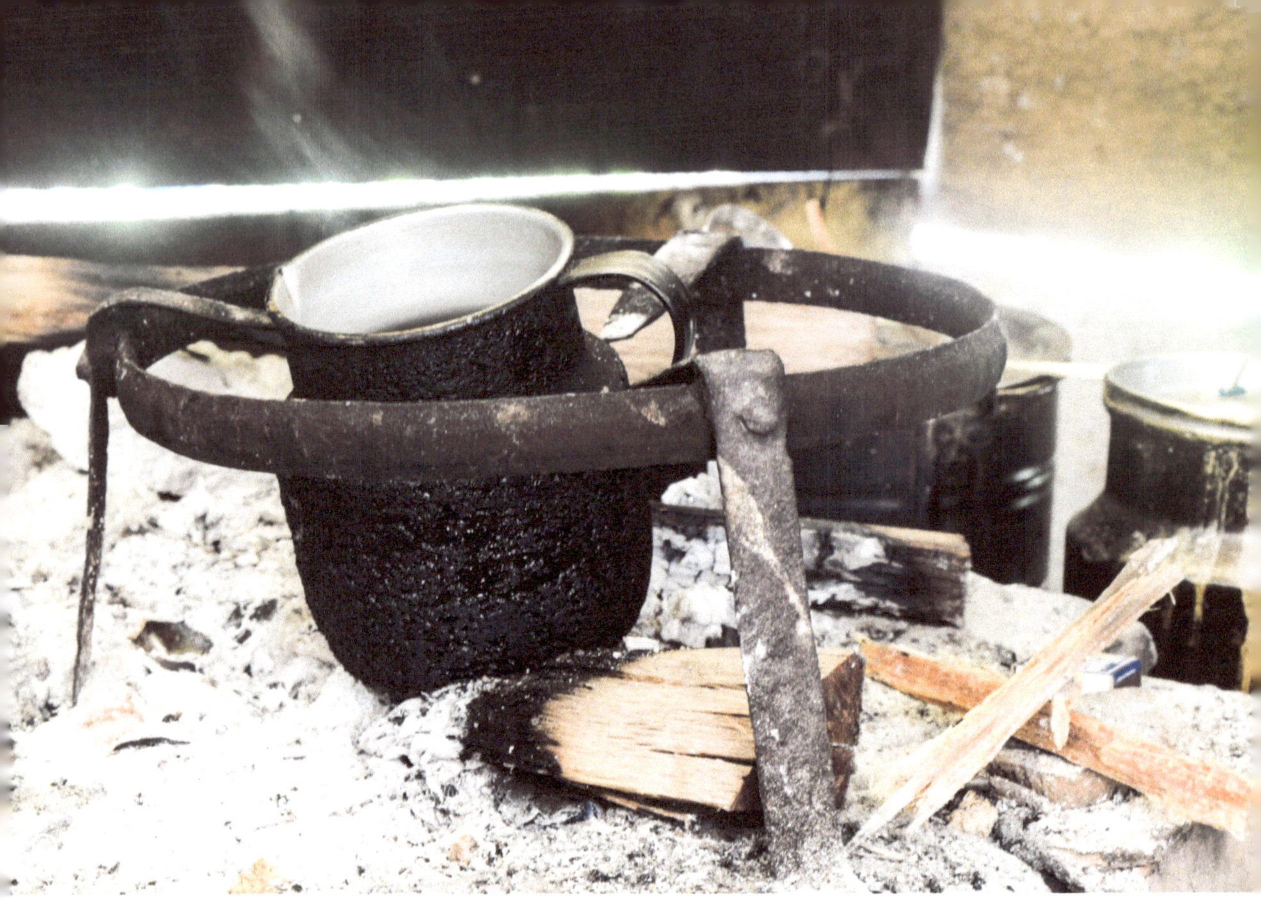

Comal & Tortillas

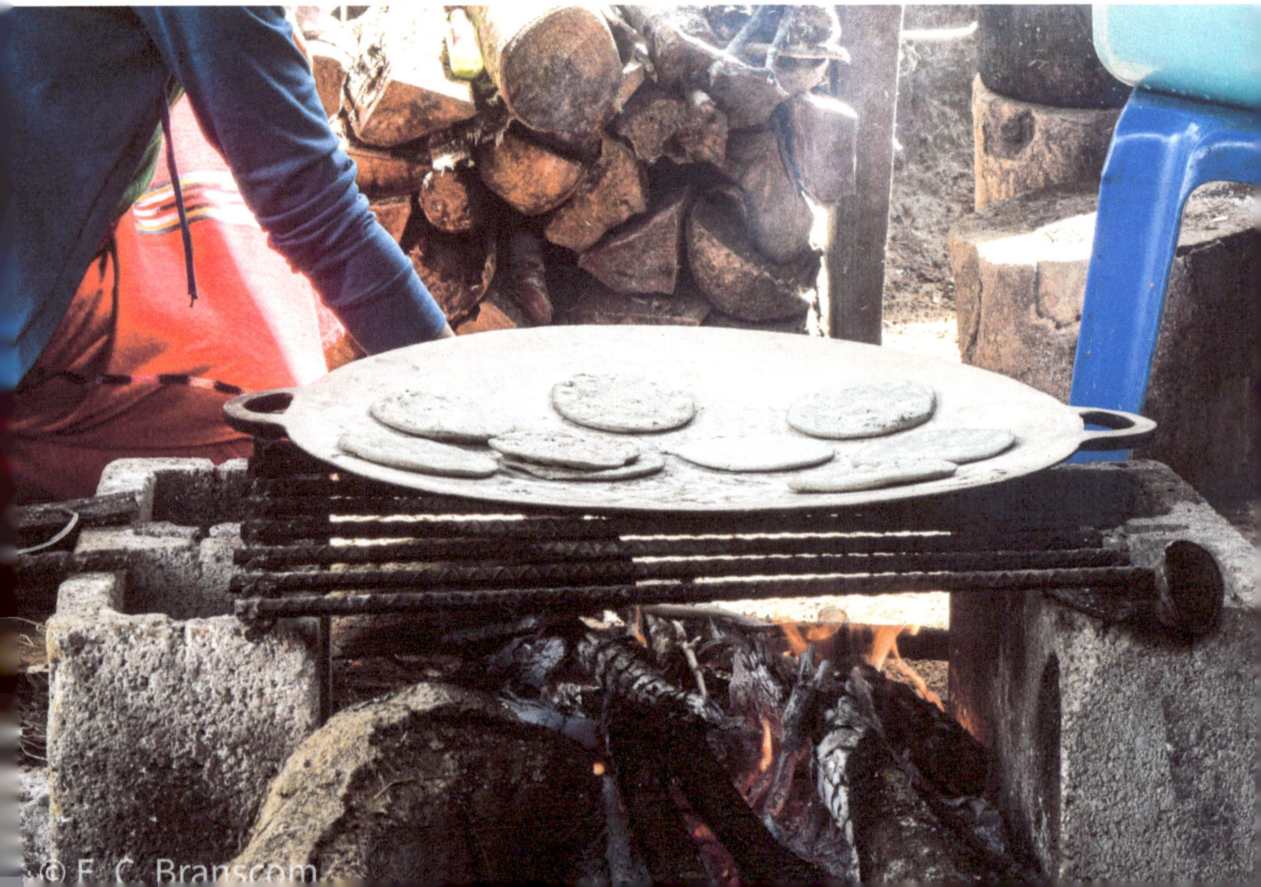

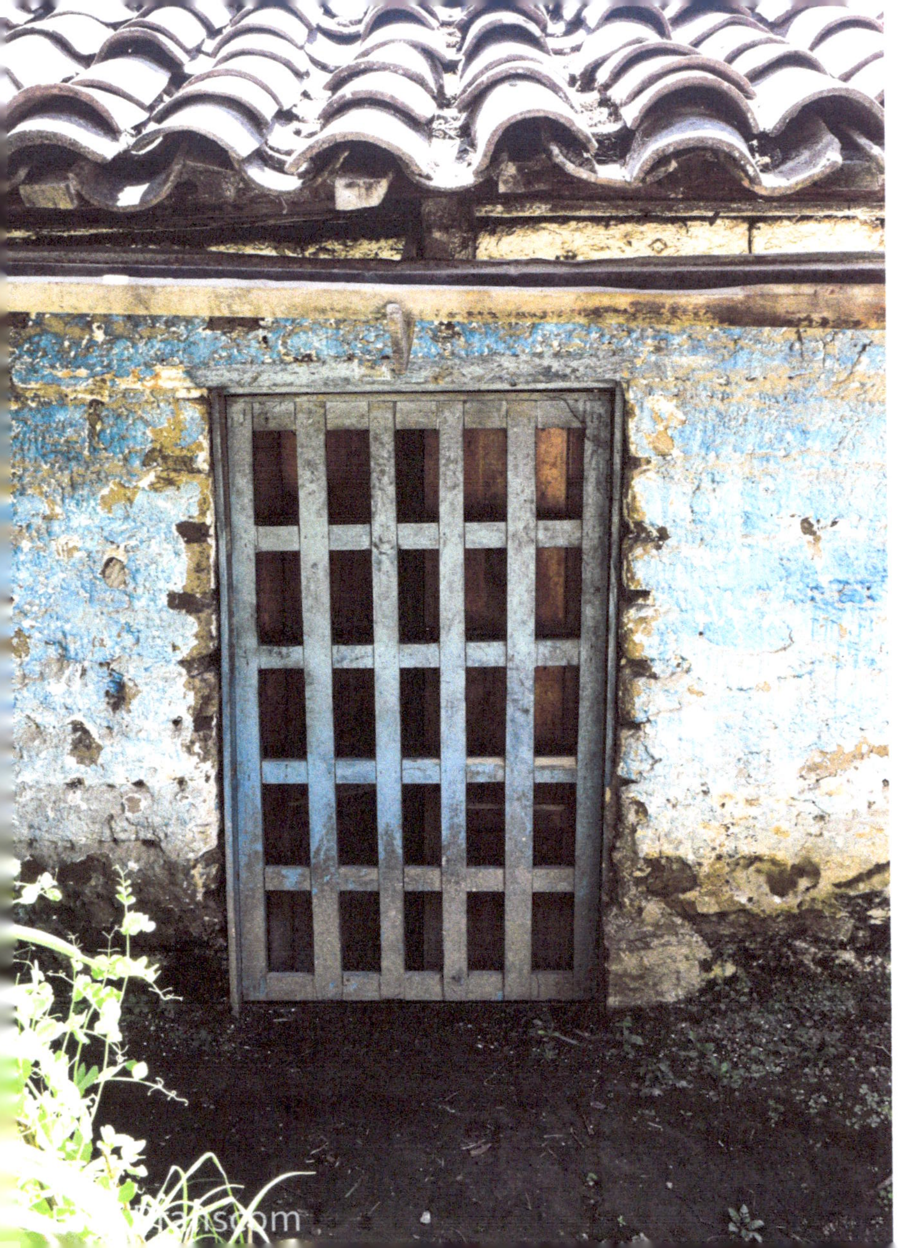

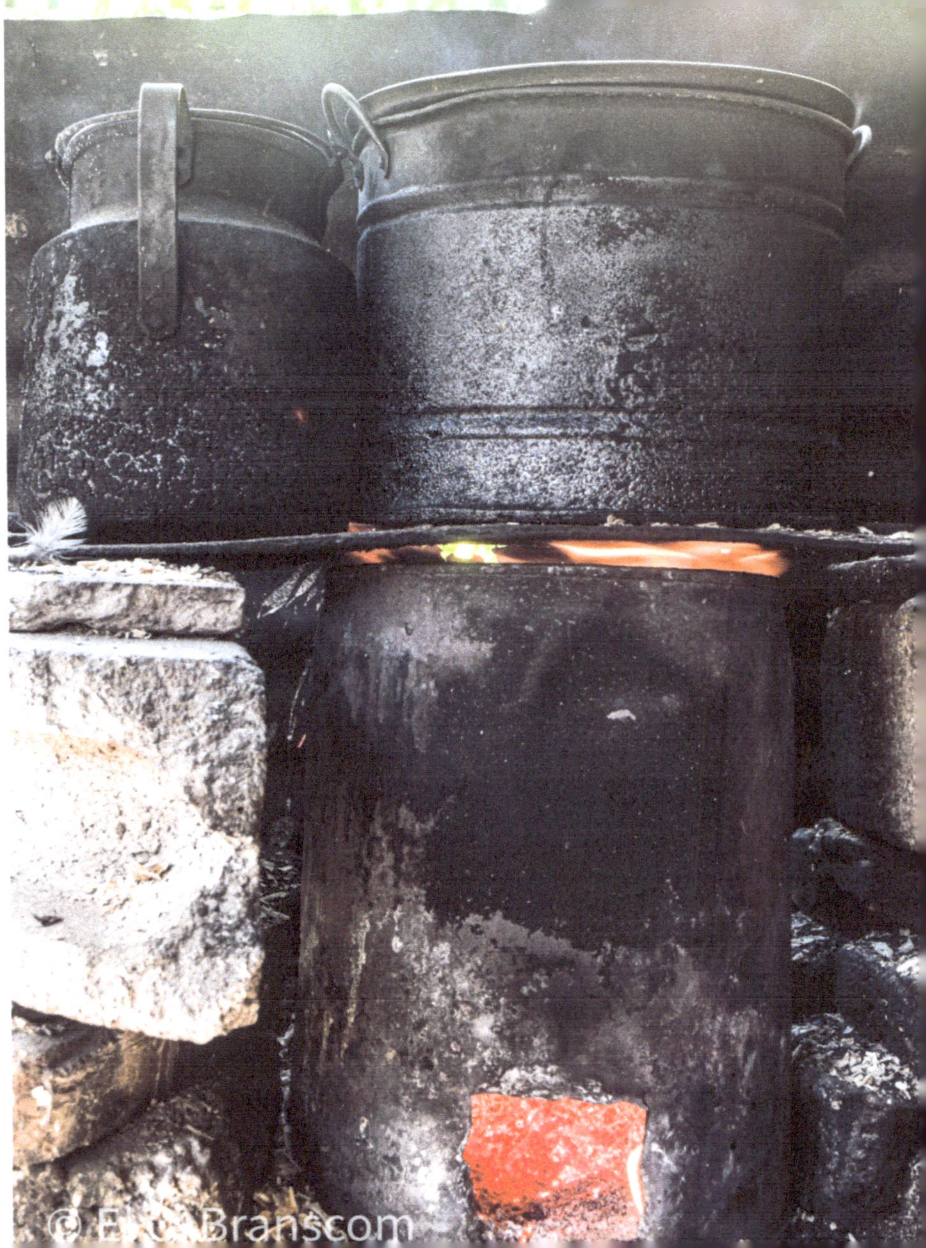

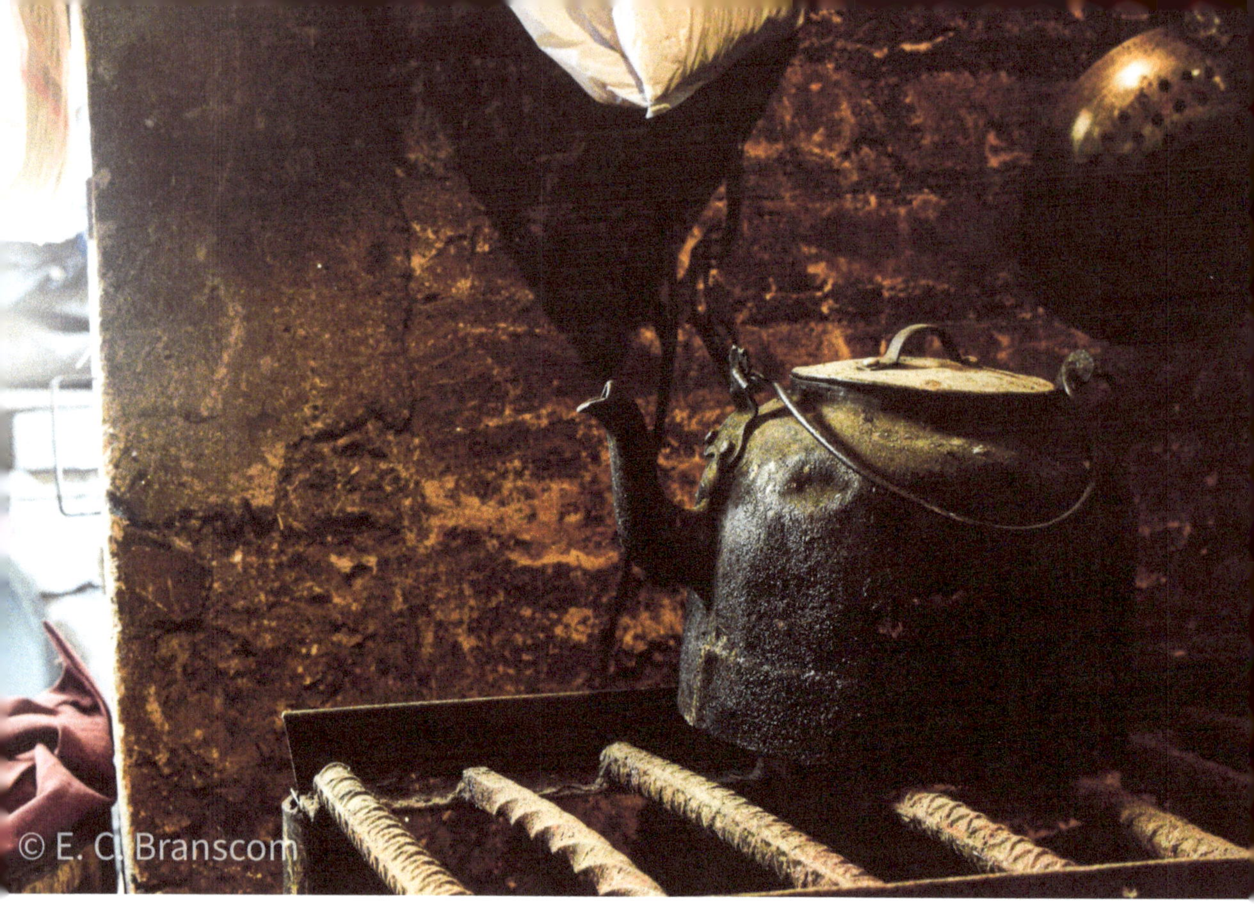

Home instruments saw in my trip to Ixil community in Guatemala (2,018)

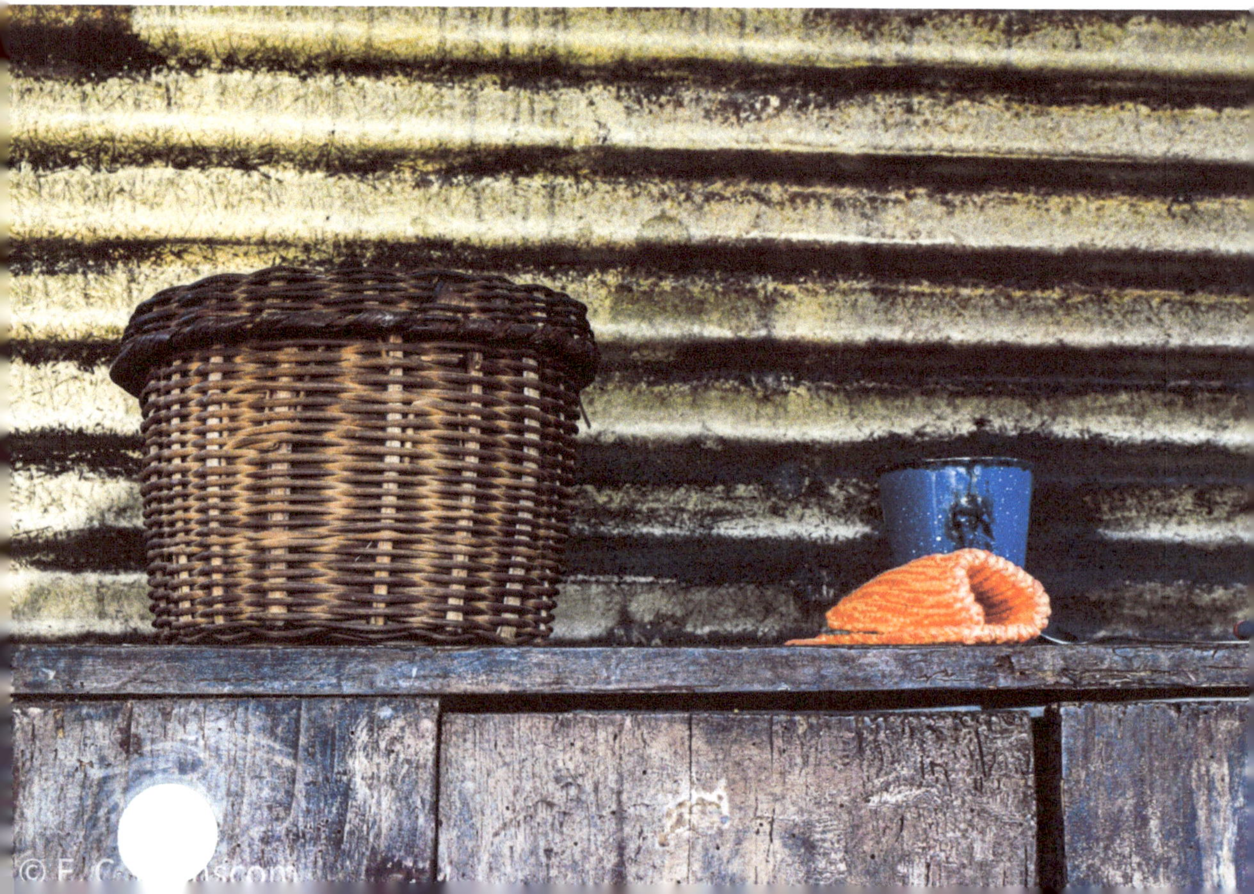

Guatemala 2,018

C. Branscom

DESIGNED & CREATED BY

E.C. Branscom

Edition: November 2022

All rights reserved. In accordance with the U.S. Copyright Act, the scanning, uploading, and electronic sharing of any part of this book without the permission of the author is the unlawful piracy and theft of the author's intellectual property. If you would like to use material from the book (other than for review purposes), prior written permission must be obtained by contacting the author. Thank you for your support of the author's right.

Printed in the USA

See more of the artist at:
www.mipigmento.com

ISBN: 9798361566419
Imprint: Independently published

Copyright © 2022 E.C. Branscom
All rights reserved.

www.ingramcontent.com/pod-product-compliance
Lightning Source LLC
Chambersburg PA
CBHW051219220526
45473CB00003B/1094